June 30th 1970

Dad,
Bill and I
want to thank you
for all your help
Love
Judy & Bill

INVESTING IN CLOCKS AND WATCHES

INVESTING

P.W. Cumhaill

 Clarkson N. Potter, Inc.

Publisher   NEW YORK

IN CLOCKS
AND

WATCHES

Produced by Design Year Book Limited, 21 Ivor Place, London N.W.1.
Published by Clarkson N. Potter Inc. New York
Text set by Harrison & Sons (Westminster) Limited, 20/22 Bedfordbury, London W.C.2.
Jackets printed by Weather Oak Press Limited, Graphic House, Lower Essex Street, Birmingham 5.
Colour pages printed by Wass, Pritchard & Company Limited, 11 Paul Street, London E.C.2.
Colour origination by L. Van Leer & Company N.V. of Amsterdam.
Printed and bound by Jarrold & Sons Limited, Cowgate, Norwich.
© Design Year Book Limited 1967.
Art Director: Ian Cameron.
House Editor and Designer: Tom Carter.
First published 1967.

Printed in England.
Library of Congress Catalog Card No. 67/24608

The colour photographs in this book are reproduced by kind permission of the Victoria and Albert Museum (pages 18, 35, 72, 90, 125, 126, 143), the Fitzwilliam Museum, Cambridge (pages 53, 54, 107) and the Usher Art Gallery, Lincoln (pages 17, 36, 71, 89, 108, 144).

Colour photography by Peter Parkinson.

All black and white illustrations are reproduced by kind permission of Sotheby & Co., and Christie, Manson & Woods Limited with the exception of those by courtesy of the Victoria and Albert Museum (page 37), the Ashmolean Museum, Oxford (page 64), the Usher Art Gallery (page 112) and the Wallace Collection (pages 111, 115, 119, 139, 140, 141, 146, 147, 148, 149, 153).

CONTENTS

Where prices are given for articles illustrated they have been estimated on the basis of public auction: no such estimate is possible for shop prices as too many factors may be involved. Higher prices are not necessarily an indication of profiteering.

In many cases the figures are quoted in pairs: the first is an estimate of the price ten years ago and the second is the probable price today.

Sums in United States dollars are not necessarily exact conversions from the sterling figures as some clocks and watches will fetch a different price on the American market.

INTRODUCTION

What does investing mean? Certainly in acquiring objects an outlay of cash is usually involved, but this is not the end of it. Time and patience are also needed, both to track down future purchases and to evaluate past acquisitions. Nor are all the benefits directly financial. Any good collection is almost in itself a form of publicity, with who knows what hidden profit. Many of the old patrons were probably in fact investing in collections which would provide visible evidence of their wealth, impress their competitors and inspire the confidence of their associates or possible clients.

However, many people seem to regard the financial side of collecting with distaste. They are happy enough to pick up a bargain, but shudder at the thought of an actual profit. Indeed, when for one reason or another collections come to be dispersed, their owners are often shocked by the high prices fetched and feel that the market must have gone mad; but of course much of the price rise is due to the change in the value of money. Collecting provides a hedge against inflation and currency devaluation, but this should be thought of as a fringe benefit rather than the first objective. The main aim behind any kind of collection should never be profit. That is the province of the full time dealer. Many amateurs have tried collecting for gain, often on the basis of random and uninformed buying, and have expected too much too soon. Fingers may get burnt as a result. While they may make money on a few pieces, probably picked up by accident, the bulk remains on their hands. Sadly, they may never know where they went wrong, and so become convinced that they have been swindled by the trade at both ends, first by

All things being equal Thomas Tompion's clocks will fetch the highest prices. As always the beginner should consult the experts before buying as it is rare for even a suspect clock to fetch less than £750, $2,100 and a good one can easily go to twenty times that price. As with anything that can be connected with a famous artist or craftsman the investment is safe but the growth rate may vary from year to year.

The ornamental aspect of this clock entirely outweighs the timekeeping function and it is doubtful that it should be considered as a clock at all. It could never be thought of as a horological investment. As a matter of interest the world record price for a clock is claimed by one of these porcelain confections!

Most of these clocks were made in the first quarter of the 19th Century. They are more like scientific instruments than clocks. In addition to the time the main dial shows the month and date. The subsidiary lunar dial is conventional. The left hand dial shows the time of sunrise and sunset. The one on the right shows the difference between mean time and solar time. The price of such clocks is governed by the maker, the complexity of the dial, and the escapement but it is most unlikely to be below £1,500, $4,200.

being asked too high a buying price, and then by being refused a sale. Stock is the dealers' lifeblood and without it they cannot survive, but they are not going to be held to ransom: if they in turn cannot see a reasonable chance of a profit, why should they buy?

The acquisition of antiques and works of art inevitably involves a capital outlay. Only the rich can afford to throw money away. While there is certainly no need to make a loss, it must be remembered that most objects have little intrinsic value and rely for the price that they will fetch on fashion or emotional appeal. Those rarities that are beyond the vagaries of the market change hands for figures which place them well out of the ordinary collector's concern. In this, as in any field, knowledge is the real key to successful investment: luck may make a valuable contribution, largely however in providing the right circumstances of time and place. Certainly people who have discovered bargains in ignorance have sometimes had the added good fortune of finding an honest purchaser, but it happens rarely. One hears of the successes, and collectors too will talk about the one that got away, but few are ready to admit that their judgement may have been wrong. The reverse is true of the dealers. They talk as if they had never bought a bargain in their lives; even if something was cheap there was something wrong with it. The trade, they say, is going to the dogs; it will never be the same as in the old days; they are thinking of giving it up. But the true dealer does not often give up. His trade is his way of life. Collecting is the same, and the biggest dividends are the pleasures of building and living with collections, of studying a chosen subject, and of pursuing new acquisitions.

Investing in antiques need not be left entirely to the specialist and the expert: you may decide, even with a very modest start, to furnish or decorate your house with them. If you avoid the traps of fashion you should from time to time be able to sell a piece for a price that will buy something better without great additional outlay. But in forming a collection to be lived with, the secret lies in buying with the heart and not with the head. Never tie up too much capital: if you need funds suddenly you will realise that a forced sale produces little profit. The danger of this almost random method of buying is that it may lead soon enough to the real collector's interest in the particular rather than the general, but the danger is offset by the advantages of becoming a specialist and the benefits of specialised knowledge. However, while this must usually come from books in the first instance, these are no more than the expression of someone else's opinions and they can only serve as a guide. In the words of Francis Quarles: 'Let the greatest part of the news thou hearest be the least part of what thou believest, lest the greatest part of what thou believest be the least part of what is true.'

Antiques bought for furnishing and decorating are almost certain to prove profitable investments. The rate of depreciation of new furniture is exceptionally high as few people buy furnishings second hand, especially in the higher price ranges. With antiques this rarely happens and therefore their real price is the difference between the price paid and the cost of a similar modern article. An immediate profit on any investment is of course very unlikely. If it was bought at auction other people with similar interests will have been competing for it as well as the trade. If it is put up for sale again a few months later one will be lucky to find anyone prepared to go to a figure approaching the previous under-bid. If it was brought from a dealer he is unlikely to take it back at the same price, and it would be unreasonable to expect him to. An estimate of the dealer's profit margin has to be made and discounted from any calculations, as any object must make up this amount before the investment can begin to show a profit.

There is a brighter side. Sometimes, even before an auction sale is over, one may be approached and asked to take a profit on an object just bought. Someone may have missed a lot or want a single item out of a mixed lot. This can happen, and it does more often than one might think.

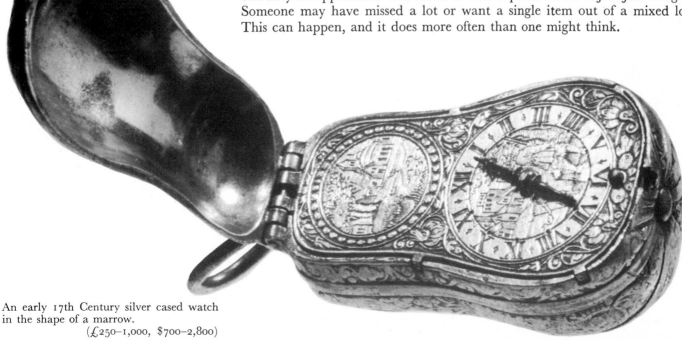

An early 17th Century silver cased watch in the shape of a marrow.
(£250–1,000, $700–2,800)

INVESTING IN HOROLOGY

Knowledge of the market is something that cannot be learnt from books, and, except in some specialist fields, lists of prices are of little use unless they have been compiled personally after looking at specimens and where possible attending auctions. A good valuer or dealer does not rely on printed lists, but makes his estimates on the knowledge of who is buying what. In time a collector acquires the same knowledge. But obviously he must start buying while he is still a novice. How can he protect himself? The safe way is to find a specialist dealer. This is not **easy** as they are a vanishing race, especially those who hold moderately priced stocks to suit the collector with a small capital. Many of the smaller shops are kept by someone with a particular bent, who will help the beginner who has the right approach. He is, after all, a prospective customer. Remember, however, that someone with a living to make cannot be expected to waste his time. He will also expect a certain loyalty, but in return may keep an eye open for objects which he thinks will be of interest. No one should try to fight the trade or try to tell them their business: nor should goods be asked for on approval so that another dealer can be consulted. If a second opinion is wanted, it is best to ask if an expert can be called in, but the buyer should not do this unless he knows the dealer very well indeed. If a bad buy can be proved in fact and is not just a matter of opinion, it should be returned and the reception given will show whether it would be wise to take custom elsewhere. Finally, opinions about dealers should not be expressed. Most of this also applies in the case of sale rooms, which are usually willing to suggest prices but cannot be used to provide free valuations. Nor do they object to experts being sent to view the sales.

The actual prices fetched at auction, with the names of the buyers, should be noted in the catalogue and compared with estimates made beforehand. After the sale it is worth analysing any great difference in prices. The faces of buyers and underbidders will in time become familiar, and, although some bids are commissions, it will soon be fairly clear who is buying. Sale prices will not necessarily relate to shop figures. Some shops work on a fixed mark up, but most do not. Buying at auction is entirely a matter of bidding, but the bidder without a limit fixed firmly in his mind may easily lose his head. When it is impossible to attend the sale a written bid can be left with the auctioneer, or someone else commissioned to buy. Even an apparently low bid may get a bargain. The greatest attraction of the auction room is the uncertainty which the human factor produces. An incomplete piece may go for a high price because two people know where the rest is; the prices may be low because the dealers are overstocked or at another sale. It may even be the weather. But these are exceptions, and for the rest of the time saleroom prices reflect the general state of the trade.

Markets are the third source of supply. There may be a chance of a good investment, as bargains can be found and there is always the pleasure of haggling. Knowledge is more important here than anywhere else. Buyers with particular interests will soon get to know which dealers are likely to have their goods. They should be visited first. They will have been round the market long before their customers, but they may have overlooked something. It is safest to buy the best that can be afforded: cheap goods, as opposed to bargains, are never satisfactory and it is better to come home empty handed than with something that is not wanted. Acquiring the object is only the beginning of the process of investment. It must be properly housed for protection, it may need repairs or restoration, and there is insurance to be considered. Once these mundane things are arranged it can be given its due attention. Attributions should be checked, similar pieces located and where possible actual comparisons made and recorded. Museums will give opinions but are forbidden to comment on values: they also have different specialities and may have particular hours for consultation. A written application for an appointment, stating the aim of the visit, is the best approach. Where a personal visit is impracticable all available information should be sent, even if it seems irrelevant. At least one photograph should be included if possible: a photographic record of any collection, or its most important pieces, is valuable if only for identification and comparison. In addition it provides material for police and assessors if anything is lost or damaged.

As the collection is built up dealers and other collectors may have an interest in buying one or more of its treasures, and will make an offer which can be

These English cases are usually loosely called 'Battersea' enamel without any reference to the latest books on English enamels. The enamel is based on copper and the frames are of gilt brass. Naturally the correct identification of the factory may influence the price but these watches are still relatively cheap.

(£7–30, $20–80)

These beetle watches come in two types and are not to be confused with the early 19th Century ones which had verge movements winding through the dial. This one was made early in the second half of the century and the movement is wound by the button at the head of the beetle, the later ones have the winding at the other end. The stones are diamonds. It is only recently that any notice has been taken of these later form watches so that no significant comparative figures can be quoted. Today they will fetch about £250, $700, the exact price will depend on condition and the number and quality of the stones.

The price of this watch will not vary much from others like it but the engine-turning under the blue enamel is cut on a straight-line engine, which is less common than the circular pattern.

(£150–300, $450–900)

The coloured-gold, floral spray is typical of the 1820's. The excellent condition is due to the protective glass. The outline of the case is unusual but would have little influence on the price.

(£25–75, $65–170)

Opposite
Top

The portrait watch 'par excellence'. Few such watches of the 17th Century exist in any form. Another portrait watch of the same period but with a difference in secondary decoration has been sold within the last ten years at a figure close to £5,000, $14,000. Today, who knows? The artist is not known but the exterior of the case and the dial bear some resemblance to the other cases attributed to Henri Toutin who was working in Paris from 1636.

Centre
The decoration on this watch case has been incorrectly described as 'cloisonné': this can be seen to be wrong as the colours are not separated by gold. This also eliminates the possibility of its being ordinary champ-levé. The problem of what it actually is remains. Is the gold in the decoration part of the case or has it been applied? Whatever the technique this case is probably unique and would command an unique price.

Bottom left
This is the type of enamel often attributed to the Toutin family. The truth of this attribution remains to be proved, but these cases were never cheap nor are they likely to depreciate. Any estimate of price, however, would be guesswork.

Bottom right
There is no evidence to suggest that this watch is not of the same period as the last (about 1650). Yet there is a visible difference in style which might indicate a later date, and there is a line of gold separating the picture from the decoration of the band. It is doubtful whether it would fetch quite such a high price.

This page
Top left

Early 17th Century repoussé cases are rare to start with. A religious scene makes it rarer. No comparative price is possible but £1,250, $3,500 would not be unreasonable. As this type of watch is probably only about 1″ in diameter it could easily be overlooked on a tray of oddments and might also be misdated.

Bottom left
The mid 19th Century engraved case has not yet come into its own. Many years will pass before the silver cases are collected and the gold ones are possibilities. The pictorial variety are the obvious choice. Either scenic views, historic scenes or portraits. The paintings and prints from which these were copied are almost given away for nothing: as they rise so will the watches. Ten years ago these watches hardly fetched their break-up value. Today they rarely go over £25, $70.

Right
A mid-17th Century silver case engraved with a perpetual calendar. The chain, seal and folding crank-key are probably original and certainly contemporary. The seal could make a difference to the price when the arms are identified. The price will, to some extent depend on the maker but it is almost certainly an English watch.
(£150–300, $450–850)

accepted, raised or refused. The proceeds of a sale can be ploughed back and new acquisitions made. When only a few pieces have to be sold they can be offered to one's regular dealer, but now it is he who has to be quoted a price. If he makes a counter-offer which is unacceptable, the goods can be taken somewhere else, but to hawk them round and finally sell for less than the first offer is the way to lose a friend. If the whole collection is concerned it can be offered to a dealer entire or sent to a saleroom with appropriate notes to help in cataloguing. If the collection is extensive the auctioneers may quote special terms and, if necessary, make an advance. Provided that its value does not depend on fashionable appeal it is sure to show a profit on the original outlay; there will have been no dividends except a great deal of tax-free pleasure, and there is the danger that one will start all over again.

For the serious collector of clocks and watches the first step is to join either the Antiquarian Horological Society in the United Kingdom, the National Association of Watch and Clock Collectors in America or the Freunde Alte Uhren in West Germany; preferably all three. Membership of the British Horological Institute in London provides access to its Ilbert Library. By joining these societies collectors can get to know each other, learn the names of dealers and have the chance of visiting some museums and private collections under conditions not normally allowed to the public. They all have their own publications; in addition the Italian journal *La Clessidra* contains fairly regular antiquarian articles. New books and occasional articles in other magazines are usually reported in the society journals. For reference G. H. Baillie's *Watchmakers and Clockmakers of the World* is indispensable, together with a book on hallmarks. Other books will be needed according to particular interests: the *Bibliographie de la Mesure du Temps*, published by Editions Tardy of Paris, has a subject index, and if it is interleaved it can be kept up to date by the insertion of reviews and publishers' lists.

For the non-specialist, whose aim is to find a few antique clocks for household use, with investment a second consideration, the main criterion is whether they look right in the surroundings of his home. Despite all the various tastes in furnishing the inevitable and apparently irreversible trend is towards a decrease in living space. It follows that the smallest clocks tend to have the highest prices and the greatest chance of appreciation. But even if it is a piece of furniture a clock is still a clock and may turn out to be an investment, and the usual questions still apply. Is it all it seems to be, or have the case and the movement been married? Perhaps decoration has been added to make it look pretty or the case has been stripped to make it look old. Has a late case been lacquered? Are there spare holes in the movement? No clock will be completely unscathed after some two centuries of use, but at least it should be more or less whole and capable of going. The case should be examined to see whether it is all of a piece, and its date estimated. The dial should fit the outline of the hood or door and should show the name of a maker who was working in the appropriate period. It is advisable to check for any large unfilled holes in the frontplate in case the dial does not belong to the movement, although this is an unlikely marriage. All this applies to the clock in the £50–200, $140–560 range: those above that level are best checked by an independent expert unless they are bought from an established specialist shop and with an invoice giving a full description. The higher the price, the greater is the incentive to make successful marriages and even to provide an entirely new case.

Today it takes a good deal of experience to be able to find a clock for under £50, $140 that is a good investment, particularly if it is a spring driven type. Low priced 'Grandfathers' are a different matter: certainly some will appreciate, but which ones they are can only be a guess. 8 day clocks in mahogany cases and with brass dials should be fairly safe if they are original throughout and not too large. The best of the 30 hour variety are the earliest, if possible with a brass dial, a lantern movement and a case made of anything but oak. They do, however, have to be wound every day and this may become tedious. To succeed in this lower priced field it is essential to develop at least some of the specialist collector's knowledge, but it is impossible to

An early 17th Century watch in a silver-gilt case. These animal 'form' watches have almost vanished from the market. In 1950 such a watch was bought for £3.10.0, $10.80. In 1954 the current price was £300, $840. Today, who knows, but over £2,000, $5,600 is probable.

recommend a speciality. Everyone has his own likes, and would do better to follow his natural preferences than to force himself into what seems to be a profitable direction. One of the great attractions of horology is its variety. It is the combination of art and technology, and much of it is still unexplored. There are many opportunities for the newcomer to become an expert in a previously little known branch of the field.

Many good clocks are ruined by ignorance or neglect. Wooden cases and movements need steady temperature and humidity. The ideal of 70° Fahrenheit at 50% is rarely practical without air conditioning, but at least any sudden changes should be avoided. Central heating produces a dry atmosphere which causes wood to shrink, warp and split, veneer to lift and joints to come apart. Oil dries up more quickly, and the clock wears faster. Clocks on mantelpieces may suffer in the same way, while those in direct light are also liable to become bleached. Some of the repairs to loose joints or mouldings and veneers that have lifted will need expert attention, but others can be done at home. In either case they must be done, as otherwise they can only get worse. Bubbles in veneer and excessive warping are best left to professionals. Case repairs cannot be hurried. The basic rules are never to replace a screw with a larger one and never to reglue a joint without first cleaning it. An extra layer of glue will simply help to keep the pieces apart, not together. Modern synthetic glues are not advisable unless they are water soluble: it may all need to be dismantled again.

Most straightforward movement repairs, including cleaning and resilvering the dial, are within the scope of the intelligent amateur and there are several useful books on the subject. Clocks must always be taken to pieces for cleaning, and kept free of cleaning solutions and polishes containing ammonia. The unrelieved stress lines in old hammer-hardened brass plates can be attacked by the ammonia and cracks may develop. This is unlikely to happen, but it is better to be safe. The degree of cleaning is a matter of personal preference: some people like a mirror finish, others just want it clean. With movements too, major repairs and restorations should be put in the hands of an expert, and one who has a feeling for antiques. The finest craftsman in the world may have no idea of the various techniques and finishes appropriate to different clocks and watches. It is not worth skimping repairs. A good repairer is worth his weight in gold, and a top class restorer is beyond price. A bad workman can easily ruin a good clock, while an artist may transform even a wreck into something of value. Surely he deserves a share of the profit.

Clocks and watches that are in use should be cleaned and oiled at least once every five years. People may say that they have had a clock for forty years and it has never needed cleaning, but all that they mean is that it is still going. When it eventually makes a very expensive noise they will probably cry bloody murder if the repair estimate is over £5, $14. The extent of restoration, like cleaning, is a matter of taste, and there is a curious anomaly here. There are some people trying to make genuine antique clocks look new, while others are working even harder to make new fakes look old. Over the years any clock will have been repaired. Holes will have been bushed and new parts made as the old wore out, and the escapement will probably have been changed. In extreme cases the whole movement may have been replaced. At the time when this was done the clocks were not valuable antiques but simply old clocks and the repairers worked in their own style without any thought of copying the original. If an anchor escapement was substituted for the verge it was because it was easier to make, not because it was more efficient. Repeating trains, alarm work and maintaining power were removed as they were no longer needed, and certainly not as acts of vandalism. To the historian of horology these are the scars of time, with the same significance as stratification to the archaeologist: to most collectors they are blemishes to be removed as soon as possible. The two viewpoints are irreconcilable and, as the point at issue here is the increase in value, the advice must regrettably be to restore.

These remarks on movements apply more generally. Metal cases should be cleaned and given a coat of lacquer. Gilt cases and silvered dials must never be cleaned with abrasive polishes. If they have to be cleaned at home, soap and water is the best means. The case must be completely dismantled first, and afterwards rinsed thoroughly and dried in warm boxwood sawdust. If it is not stripped down it may corrode and go green in places. Enamel cases need protection from accidental blows and clocks with revolving rosettes or decorative porcelain flowers have to be guarded from the dangers of dusting. The problem with watches is mainly one of storage or display, or both, and much will depend on the value of the collection and the opinions of its insurers. With glass fronted display cases the choice may be between a type specified by the insurance company or an uneconomical premium. The minimum requirement for a glazed case is that it should be dustproof and have struts to keep the lid open. Lights should be kept out of the case, or it should be well ventilated. Oak must never be used in the construction. If there is a lining it should be fixed with a paste or glue that will not turn acid with age. Plasticine has a tendency to mark cases and so should not be used for supports. With any luck the collection will soon grow too large to be put on display as a whole and part will have to go into drawers or boxes. Boxes can be made up as they are needed, preferably with constant length and breadth but varying depth, while with a chest-of-drawers the size of the storage unit is inflexible and may turn out to be inconvenient. Perhaps the most logical system is a series of boxes stored singly on adjustable shelves: this avoids the inevitable problem of getting one box out of the bottom of a pile. Whatever containers are used, they should be lined with velvet or baize, and separate compartments made for every watch by fitting dividers which can be removed when the cloth is brushed. Cases are protected from wear if the watches are placed to rest on the glass. This is especially important with enamelled types, since their value is almost entirely dependent on good condition. Enamel is also sensitive to sudden temperature changes and has been known to shatter when these are severe. Safe and cabinet doors should be opened gently and left ajar for ten to fifteen minutes. Explosions are rare but at today's prices one is too many. Early watches are unlikely to be kept going but it is best to have them cleaned and not oiled: the old oil will have become gummy and acid with age and may cause corrosion. Watch cases are relatively easy to clean except when they are set with gem stones, paste or pearls. Those should be taken to a jeweller.

Increasing the value of a collection and eventually selling it have their own techniques. A little sales promotion helps even the best clocks and watches. Attention should always be drawn to any particular points of interest, or they may be overlooked. The interest itself may be artistic or technical or it may be simply associated. This may be the most difficult to assess and often brings the least return for the greatest effort. The most obvious association is with the original owner: on timepieces made before 1700 the only evidence may be in the form of arms or a crest engraved on the case, or less satisfactorily,

The filigree outer-case can be thought of as a separate item. The price will depend on the metal, the design and the condition. Although the silver case is much rarer than the gold, there is a vast difference in the relative price. A silver one might be bought for £40, $100; gold, £150, $450. At least this amount should be added to the price of the watch if it is contemporary.

There may seem to be an over-emphasis on the dating of cases but whereas a movement may be dated by checking the maker's name, no such easy method exists for cases which often have no hall-mark, let alone a signature. The agreement in date between case and movement can make a big difference to the soundness of an investment. The general impression given by this case is, 'second half of the 17th Century, pendant possibly replaced, clock-watch or alarum, probably about 1670–80'. This impression is given by the rosettes in the centre, the way the 'serpent' spirals through the decorative foliage and the inclusion of the little dogs. Naturally the price will depend on what the case contains.

on seals attached to it. Inscriptions referring to the original owner are exceptionally rare, and many of them are suspect. After 1700 heraldry is still important, but there is also a chance of reliable documentary evidence from bills and accounts. However, this is rare except in the case of the A-L. Breguet productions. Such identification is a valuable aid to dating and, even if the actual owner cannot be traced, the record of an object in a book or the catalogue of an earlier collection can bring some financial benefit by providing a proof of authenticity. If no direct association can be found, similarity to other objects in private or public collections should be noted. The great danger of the association gamble is the temptation to cheat by trying to transform possibility into actuality. Facts should be proved beyond all reasonable doubt and if this is impossible the similarities alone should be recorded and the buyer left to form his own final opinion. In many cases apparently positive identification is given by illustrations and descriptions in books or catalogues, but the descriptions themselves are seldom conclusive unless they quote the maker and serial number. They are rarely sufficiently complete and often inaccurate, as can be shown by a comparison of the various differing descriptions of a single clock—even when these have been taken from a common source without direct examination of the object. There is no short cut to the discovery of secondary association. Books and catalogues have to be checked, but in time certain sources come to be familiar, and if the maker is known, Baillie's list may give information about the location of other examples.

The stackfreed has already been noted as an example of what provides technical interest, as have the various methods of enamelling. These are obvious points and are easy to recognise, but most technical details must be related to date or maker or place of manufacture. Here the beginner is at a disadvantage. He knows for instance that the verge is an old form of escapement, while the lever is modern. This is liable to suggest that the verge watch of 1780 is more valuable than one of the same date with a lever escapement. The same argument applies to jewelling, which would be remarkable in an early 18th Century watch made anywhere but in England, but the beginner may expect watches to be jewelled and will not recognise the importance of its presence or absence. At first it is better to think that everything is important until it is proved one way or the other than to miss something, and it is certainly better to be thought ignorant than foolish. Although few clocks and watches are unique, they can be important because of the existence of some detail which has to be isolated and identified. This can be a tedious process with early specimens, but from 1700 patent specifications are available, at least for such innovations as were registered.

The artistic side of horology has been more or less overlooked, largely because there has been no overall review of the various forms of decoration that occur within particular types. The work that has been done on the identification of designs has usually been confined to making comparisons with the pattern books of Etienne Delaune or, more rarely, Simon Gribelin. The possible rarities are not yet highly priced and their value is judged simply on their condition, so that there is no way of predicting the possible financial advantage of research in this field. A watch must not only be found to be rare, it must be proved to be rare. This leads on to the question of how to enhance the value of a collection after all the research has been done. Publicity can be obtained by writing articles based on one's findings, by giving lectures and by making the collection available for others to inspect. It may give rise to offers of objects for sale and requests for illustrations for books, and these should be treated as far as possible on a commercial basis, being part of the benefit of making an investment. Collectors should have their own photographs and charge reproduction fees while keeping the copyright, unless they think that the resulting publicity is return enough. In any case one should be consistent. If some pay and not others there will eventually be bad feeling that may undo all the good that has been achieved. Investing in clocks and watches is not quite the same as putting money in stocks and shares which produce a dividend, because this is taxable and depends on other people's efforts. Admittedly, collections may appreciate in time through a fall in the value of money or an increase in the number of collectors and the growing scarcity of specimens, but it is better to use one's own initiative. The factor common to all investing is the ability to buy the right thing at the right price and at the right time. There can be no specific rules about this as the picture changes all the time: nor would they be useful, since they might cause a general move in one direction with a false rise in prices. Mostly, the horological market has been steadily rising with slight peaks when collections have come up for sale. It has not yet shown the great increases which have been seen in other fields. Some particular types have made spectacular gains— precision watches, especially the work of A-L. Breguet, fine enamels of all periods, automaton pieces and some well preserved early types. These gains should continue if not increase: the supply is tending to dry up as items pass into public collections from which they are unlikely to emerge, or private ones which will probably not be dispersed for some time. But as the supply diminishes there are signs that the emphasis is moving to other varieties. Watches with fine gold repoussé cases, for example, and 17th Century continental types are beginning to appreciate. The risk is greatest with the high priced watch, especially if the type has always had a high value. Early clocks and watches have been faked and restored at least since 1800, and this has led to a curious situation where over-restored items that are basically genuine can fetch less than complete forgeries which are elaborate enough to make people think that producing them would not be a commercial proposition. This can be a great advantage for the knowledgeable buyer in view of the present increase in comparative research which is tending to explode some of the standard myths and even to prove that some of the so called fakes are in fact genuine, although only part of the original fabric may remain.

Apart from the crucial individual points to be looked for in early clocks and watches there are also general comparisons which can be made: does the general appearance agree with the concept of the period? Does the style fit the supposed maker?—this is particularly important when the object has initials or punchmarks, other than those which refer to a town. Is it over-restored or over-repaired? This is a more complicated question, and the answer depends partly on how much restoration a future buyer is likely to accept, and whether any improvement can be made in the meantime. This last is itself a difficult problem; while it may be thought excusable to replace and improve a bad restoration or to restore missing parts, the process of ' de-modernization ' is, as mentioned earlier, of debatable value. Occasionally one finds items which are so incomplete as to be almost fragments: in consequence they can be bought comparatively cheaply, but what is to be done with them? On the Continent there is no difficulty, they are ' documentary pieces ' and their value is related to their rarity. This perceptive attitude has crossed neither the English Channel nor the Atlantic, where something near to completeness is required. Strangely however, movements and early cases are thought of as complete entities in themselves, and although marriages may have been made, they are usually detectable unless very well done. But an incomplete case containing an incomplete movement presents a real problem: the owner must consider how much of the original survives and act on his own feelings. If the initial cost and the probable bill for restoration are considerably less than the current market price the temptation to restore will be great. This has no real bearing on the actual buying, but is a question of ethics.

For early clocks and watches then, the requirements are: reasonable condition in accordance with their age, some agreement in the movement and decoration with contemporary pieces and, if possible, a credible provenance. To be avoided: replacements by electrotype copies or made up parts, iconographical errors and obviously unreasonable associations.

As far as price goes the watch in an enamelled case is on a par with the horological incunabula. The faker has been at work here too, with particular attention to early champlevé and basse-taille examples and some so-called Limoges enamel cases. The results are generally rather crude, seem too well preserved, and are comparable to the Renaissance jewels turned out by the same workshops for the same customers. They rarely come on the market now, and all that need be said about them is that they are usually let down either by their movements or by the construction of the cases themselves. Some of the late guilloché enamels are, to say the least, re-enamelled and are often set with diamond monograms. As they are virtually indistinguishable from the originals—if there are in fact any originals—they are unlikely to be detected except by people who recognize them from familiarity rather than from experience.

Alterations to painted enamel are usually in the form of plaques that have been added or replaced, but a very few fully enamelled and painted cases have been made and their identification is extremely difficult. Two experts will rarely agree on whether they are genuine, so that conclusive proof one way or the other is practically impossible. It seems unlikely that it will ever be more than a matter of opinion.

The main point of concern with enamels is the extent of any damage and this has a direct bearing on the value. The number of enamel watches which have survived in almost perfect condition is surprising but as these rarely come on to the market unless a collection is being broken up a certain amount of damage has to be expected and tolerated. But the price should be adjusted accordingly. Damage can be either surface scratching or partial breakage where the actual body of enamel has been broken and is missing. A scratched surface on early enamels is often not serious and can be improved with wax polish: the later Genevan enamels are covered with a clear flux and the picture or ground is seldom affected. However, the enamel on some of the early 18th Century cases is softer and large areas of the surface can be rubbed off to show the white base. There is no effective way of restoring these although they are sometimes repainted in oils or water colours and varnished. The successful restoration of missing enamel is even more difficult as the ground must be made up almost to the level of the original surface leaving only enough room for the thickness of the paint. Some repairs have been and still are done by refiring but although the results can be excellent this is an expensive process and there are few artists who are capable of carrying it out. The most vulnerable parts of the case are the areas round the pendant and near the catch. The pendant was often torn out of the case, taking part of the enamel with it: if this happened while the watch was being carried it would naturally drop and damage the opposite side. The inside of the case suffered at the same time. The contemporary method of repair was to fit gold plates over the damaged area and these were often engraved. When there was extensive damage the case might be cut into five parts, the back and the four panels of the band, and they were then fitted into specially made repoussé cases.

The small areas of missing enamel sometimes found on the backs of cases are the results of blows with a sharp instrument and reflect the changing value of these painted enamel cases. This was deliberate damage aimed at discovering whether the enamel was on gold or copper and whether it was worth buying for the small gold content.

Modern repairs by repainting are easily discovered under an ultra-violet lamp even when the colours are a perfect match. Older restorations will still smell of oil paint while the later ones which are covered with a cellulose or synthetic-resin lacquer have a different feel from the original enamel. A pendant of a later pattern may also betray a repair. In the later cases with an enamel plaque fitted into a bezel the obvious repair is to fit a completely new back and this will only be suspect when it is out of keeping with the general style of the period or type of case. Occasionally the back is replaced with a glass so that the movement is visible: it then ceases to be an enamel and its value depends on the technical rather than the decorative aspect. The amount of damage, repaired or otherwise, will help to determine what is a reasonable price, but it is as well to remember that it is becoming increasingly hard to find undamaged examples.

Enamels apart, the price of any decorative watch depends on its condition. Engraving can be retouched to some extent but little can be done with badly rubbed cast, repoussé or coloured gold decoration. The re-gilding of base metal cases is a doubtful proposition; it can rarely be done well enough to escape detection and as a general rule a re-gilt case could fetch less, particularly if it has been done electrolytically.

If the case seems satisfactory the next question is whether the movement belongs to it. This may be difficult or impossible to decide especially with enamel watches as there was an extensive export trade in cases alone. Sometimes a wrong movement can be detected through badly fitted hinges or an obvious discrepancy between the estimated dates of case and movement. Base metal cases may give much the same problem where they have no identifying marks other than false hall-marks. These can be ridiculous. A Swiss made watch is known which is signed 'Geo. Prior, London' and intended for the Turkish market. Its copper alloy case has marks similar to those of the Goldsmiths' Hall in London and is also punched with the word *léton* (laiton = brass). Evidently the maker wanted the best of both worlds; the metal was identified to satisfy the law while he hoped that his customers would be unable to read it but would recognise the hall-marks and be impressed. Most false hall-marks are found in silver cases which are part of the variety of commercial imitations made from about 1700 onwards and aimed at a number of markets, particularly, at different periods, Holland and Russia. They were manufactured as complete watches so that there are no discrepancies between the movement and the case. Where no positive identification can be supplied by matching numbers, hall-marks or case-makers' stamps it is always advisable to check the alignment of the winding holes and the fit of the hinges and the inner and outer cases. The last point can be less important as the two cases were sometimes by different makers.

The condition of the mechanical element is also important, but becomes less so with age. Many watches made after 1700 keep reasonable time and can be worn. It is worth paying considerable attention to the completeness of the movement, and the price to be paid will depend on the estimated repair costs for both case and movement. Hands and glasses are also significant to a degree. The original glass will probably not have survived, but the replacement should be in the correct style. The same is true for the hands, although these are obviously more durable. New hands can be made to the correct design, but stocks of glasses are disappearing.

Almost the ultimate in Turkish Export Clocks with tortoiseshell veneer, gilt metal mounts and a procession with music. £1,500, $4,200 at least and likely to go up.

The non-availability of spare parts has to be faced right from the start: many people seem surprised that they cannot walk into a shop and buy parts even for later clocks and watches which were made after interchangeability had become an established practice. With the possible exception of mainsprings all replacement parts must be made by hand and are therefore expensive. This aspect of watch and clock restoration is so obvious that it is often overlooked and may cause a well laid plan to go astray. Largely for this reason the difference in price, at auction, between a watch in going order and one in need of repair seldom bears any relation to the possible cost of restoration. Generally the difference represents the cost of cleaning which will have to be done in any case as it is rare to find a watch in perfect going

This clock hardly qualifies as a skeleton clock. The front plate of the movement is a plate of glass. The bell at the bottom shows that this is indeed a clock. These come in several qualities and this will affect the price. A good example will be about £250, $900. These clocks are more likely to appreciate in value than straightforward skeletons.

order even if it is in fact mechanically complete.

All this may seem to be a gloomy picture, but it is better to underline the dangers than to create false confidence. Most clocks and watches which change hands today are authentic but, just as in any other field, there are traps for the unwary and it is always easy to lose money, especially as more and more people are becoming interested in the subject. As the number of collectors grows so there is an increase in the demand for more detailed books: this leads to more research and inevitably to the disproving of popular beliefs. Collectors in turn will become more critical and the good pieces will be the ones which appreciate in value while the doubtful items will be lucky to find a market.

This is little more than a watch movement fitted into an ornament. It is not for the investor in clocks and watches. The clocks with appled flowers are particularly dangerous for the uninitiated as the blooms were copied later as replacements. If you must buy this type of clock at least try to find one with the right movement. It will make no difference to the current price.

THE EVOLUTION
OF CLOCKWORK

The history of horology is a subject which is to a great extent controversial even today, and is anyway only of academic interest to the collector. He is unlikely to acquire clocks dating from much before the middle of the 16th Century. But a brief description of the evolution of the various types and some technical information may be useful, so that the investor can have some idea of what he is buying and where it fits into the overall picture.

As the history of clocks and watches comes to be better understood, the emphasis will fall on different types and values will change. For many years clocks supposedly made in Augsburg and Nuremberg held pride of place. Almost any early catalogue or book shows most of the early clocks as ascribed to one of these towns or, in doubtful cases, called South German. France is occasionally referred to, but England, Italy and the Low Countries are almost entirely absent. Recently the importance of the early French clocks has been realised, to the advantage of anyone who had the wit or luck to be ahead of the market. More lately still the focus has moved to Italy, and a specimen that can be ascribed to that country with any certainty has a good chance of fetching a high price. In making a correct identification a knowledge of technology is often of greater importance than a knowledge of evolution.

Clockmakers tend to be conservative and keep to the methods they learn as apprentices. So regional styles grow up and any change that does not bring with it some benefit, usually financial, is resisted. The briefest comparative study will show the differences in technique that do occur, in spite of the common complaint that all clocks, especially the early ones, are the same. The significance of these differences is largely a matter of conjecture, although in some points the picture is beginning to clear. An acquaintance with some aspects of art history is also useful to the horologist trying to identify the origin of a clock, but this comes only from a study of decoration in general and is outside the scope of this book.

The collector must learn to recognise the mechanical parts of clocks and their various purposes to be able to assess what he intends to buy. While the basic facts are comparatively simple and can be learnt easily from a book, knowledge of the finer points can come only from experience, and this can only be gained by a really careful examination of every available horological item.

Most clocks or watches made before the end of the 17th Century will originally have had a verge escapement. This is easy to recognise: the scape wheel has saw-shaped teeth set at right angles to the wheel itself which engage two pallets mounted at 90° to each other on the verge arbor. The frequency of oscillation of the verge is controlled by a balance or a foliot fixed to its upper end. The balance is a wheel with a complete or occasionally a partly cutaway rim, and in most early cases two spokes forming a diameter. Single radial spokes do occur and are almost universal in English lantern clocks. The foliot is a crosspiece mounted on edge with a series of slots to hold two weights. As the weights are moved closer to the centre the clock runs faster. In most of the earlier clocks a notched arm is attached to the frame and supports the verge by a cord. Moving the cord provides a fine regulating adjustment: as the point of suspension is moved sideways away from the central position the side thrust and increasing friction make the movement run more slowly.

The hour and quarter striking is controlled by a count wheel, a universal system up to about 1670 which remained in use on the Continent and in America for at least another two hundred years. The form of the count wheel varies: essentially it is a wheel whose rim has a series of notches separated by increasing distances. The locking lever of the striking train has a projection which rests on the rim and falls into each of the notches in turn as the wheel rotates, so that the number of blows struck depends on the distance between each notch. The count wheel is rotated by the striking train, and as the time struck depends on its position and not the time shown on the dial, the two trains can get out of synchronisation. In the open clock the position of the wheel can be seen and the striking corrected by releasing the train manually. In some cased types a hand is driven from the count wheel so that its position is shown on a dial. The striking is let off by the going train in several ways. Before about 1700 there were two main methods, though the actual point of release varied. Originally this was a pin on the great wheel, rotating once

The 'Diane de Poitiers' clock. This is a gambler's clock. Tradition has it that this clock dates from about 1547 and that it was made for Henri II to give to Diane de Poitiers. Documentary evidence shows that the clock was in existence before 1862. When it was sold it was pointed out that it was probably a 'reconstruction'. It fetched £1,550, $4,340. The attribution depends on the profusion of crowned 'H's', conjoined 'D's' and 'H's' and crescents that occur all over the clock. The refutation is largely based on the lack of exact comparative material in any form. This makes the fact that the striking train is in the upper part of the two-stage movement suspicious. The enamel dial is, at least, most unusual at this date but could be a replacement. However, lack of comparative material can act both ways, negative proof is never satisfying. The gamble lies in being able to prove that the clock did in fact, belong to Henri II which would increase the price about fourfold. Proof might be possible through the inventories. If this clock is not above suspicion it raises the question of who could afford the expense of making such a thing and for what market and when? And incidentally what else was made?

an hour. Where there was a quarter train this was controlled by four pins on the great wheel and the hours were released by the quarter train in a similar way. With this arrangement the clock could not be set to time by turning the hand: it had either to be stopped or the escapement disengaged

This cannot be considered as an ordinary crucifix clock. Everything about it is unusual, the silver mount, the enamel decoration on the figures and the set stones. It is possible that the rotating crown with the chapters engraved on a silver band is not original. The maker's name would have some influence on the price but not a great deal. No quotation is really possible but such a clock would make a very safe investment.

to let the train run free until the hand pointed to the right time. Weight driven clocks could be stopped be removing the weight, but spring clocks were fitted with a brake acting on the scape wheel. To disengage the escapement a lever was fitted to raise the verge and lift the pallets clear. While there are

The mandorla behind the Virgin is unusual and may be a later addition. Other casts from this particular model are known but the finishing can vary between bad and very good.

(£100–750, $280–2,100)

The Lyre clock was first made about 1770–80 during the reign of Louis XVI. In the early examples the movement itself acted as the bob of the pendulum, later the ring of pastes surrounding the bezel was connected to the pendulum and swung from side to side. Later still the movements were fitted with platform escapements and the ring was fixed, the clocks also became smaller. Some reproductions were made with swinging bezels.

The cases may be made of white marble or a similar stone, porcelain, usually blue, or enamel on copper in imitation of porcelain.

The price will naturally vary according to the model and the condition. A good Louis XVI lyre clock should fetch at least £250, $700 and this is still well below the peak price.

The lyre clock often has two accompanying ornaments, if these are present the price should, at least, be doubled.

some spring clocks which have the point of release in the train, this is mainly characteristic of the 'Gothic' clocks, many of which were made after 1600, not as fakes but from normal practice.

To make adjustment easier, the pin on the great wheel was replaced by a twelve pointed star wheel attached firmly to the arbor carrying the hour hand. The wheel for the hand was friction tight on the arbor so that the hand itself could be turned. This was a great improvement but the striking could still get out of synchronisation. The first of the two methods for releasing the strike uses a locking lever with a jointed end returned by gravity or a spring. The pin on the great wheel engages with the jointed end, and after taking it to the limit of its free movement raises the locking lever and frees the striking train. As this runs it lifts the lever still more until the jointed end slips over the pin and the mechanism is returned to the locking position. The points of the star wheel have the same effect as the pin: the jointed end of the lever will unlock in one direction only, so that with the star wheel system the hand can be set backwards. If it is set back too far the striking must be corrected. This system was used in all German clocks and clock watches until at least 1700.

The second release mechanism is more complicated but seems to have been used by the French, and probably the Flemish clockmakers from about 1520.

An early 17th Century clock like this is going to cost money. £3,000, $8,400 would be the minimum and £8,000, $22,500 would not be unreasonable. Prices higher than this will depend on the maker and the general condition and what is to be found on the dials on the other two sides of the clock. Inevitably such clocks gravitate towards museums and the price is going to rise steadily but at an increasing rate as time goes on.

Opposite left

This is what might be called the standard type of gilt-metal crucifix clock. The time is indicated on the rotating ball at the top of the cross. The movement in the base may have a stackfreed or a fusee and this can affect the price. The presence or absence of a maker's name or mark will also make a difference. Today's average figure would be about £500, $1,400 which shows an increase of between 5 and 6 times the average of ten years ago.

This page right

This is a more elaborate version of the preceding type with a probable increase of at least 15 per cent.

Top left

This clock could be nothing but Germanic, of the second half of the 16th Century. These clocks are less impressive than the later and more ornate tabernacle clocks and rarely fetch such high prices. This is one of the idiosyncrasies of present collectors.

(£150–650, $420–1,850)

Right

A far less common type of crucifix clock. There is no mechanical difference but the movement is much larger and it would be most surprising if a fusee movement was not being used. The pierced decoration under the glazing of the base is most unusual. Such a clock would fetch about three times the price of the gilt-metal type which would mean an increase of above 15 times in the same period.

Almost the standard 'Augsburg Tabernacle Clock'. The central disc in the dial indicates that it is an alarum although the mechanism may be missing. The two bells above the case should mean that it strikes the quarters as well as the hours. There should be two small dials on the back of the clock with irregularly spaced numerals, one numbered from 1–4 for the quarters and the other 1–12 for the hours. Although many of these clocks are collected for their decorative appeal and as examples of early 17th Century workmanship the horological investor should pay attention to the condition of the movement which will probably be of brass.

(£50–750, $140–2,100)

It was also used in England. The let off lever is not the same as the locking lever, and the strike occurs after the let off lever falls, rather than as it is being lifted. It is raised in the same way as in the first method, but moves a stop into the striking train. The locking lever lifts and frees the train, which runs for a short distance until it is relocked on the stop and is finally released when the end of the let off lever falls behind the pin of the tip of the star. The first short movement of the train is called the warning, and this type of release still remains in use. It makes quarter striking a little more difficult to arrange, and clocks of this type with a quarter strike are extremely rare, although some were made with a chime, the extra run needed for a chime making the construction that much easier.

There are both spring and weight driven clocks which strike either 1 to 6 or 1 to 24 in addition to the now standard 1 to 12. Some can be changed from one count to another. These differences can provide an indication of the clock's nationality, although usually the evidence is negative. The strike sequence will also be shown on the dial and can be considered together with it. One other important feature of some striking work is often overlooked: clocks can be found which have, or show traces of, two pins placed close together on the great wheel. The count-wheel is cut so that every hour will be struck twice, once on the hour and again a few minutes later. Present evidence shows that these were Italian and made before about 1630. The repeated strike is also found in clocks from the Franche Comté, but of a much later date. A striking system that may be found in pre-18th Century clocks, though it is normally thought of as a relatively late invention, is Grande Sonnerie, with the hour repeated after every quarter. This was certainly in use by the first half of the 16th Century and, by the beginning of the 17th, had been elaborated by the addition of a further train so that the hour itself was struck twice.

The clock dial had become almost standardised in the 12 hour form by the end of the 17th Century. Before then, various systems were in use. As the chances of finding a clock made much before 1550 are few, only dials of the following hundred years will be considered. The straightforward 12 hour dial

The figure for this Virgin clock comes from the same mould as the one on p.34 but the execution of the detail is much finer and so it might fetch a slightly higher price.

was practically universal west of the Rhine and north of the Alps; in France, Flanders, England and the Netherlands. Roman numerals were always used, and, in general, the earlier the dial, the wider the numerals are in relation to their height. In Germany, although the 12 hour system had been recognised officially for about two centuries, the dials were arranged so that they could be used for the 24 hour count, with the Arabic numerals 13 to 24 inside the Roman figures. This may have been for trade reasons, as such clocks could be used throughout Europe except perhaps near Rome where the 6 hour count continued. In Italy the 24 hours started at the end of twilight—half an hour after sunset—as it did in Bohemia and what is now known as Germany, where it was called the 'Grosse Uhr' and the 12 hour count the 'Kleine Uhr'. Manuscript evidence shows that clocks indicating the French and Italian hours were made in and around Lyons at the end of the 16th Century, but so far few have been definitely identified. Other systems occur but mostly in conjunction with the 24 hour dial.

The actual construction of clocks is divided into two forms, which may conveniently be called frame and plated: both can be spring or weight driven. The frame clock is the earlier type of construction. In these the weight drive came first, while initially the plated clocks were spring driven. It is not practical to describe the general evolution of clockwork, as there are many local differences whose significance has not yet been fully analysed. But a brief illustration of the various types and the apparent details of their development will help to give some guide to the date of a clock. The frame clock itself may have descended from a primitive form which seems to have survived into the 18th Century to be used in the Zaanse clock. This movement has three vertical bars which carry the wheels and are united at the top and bottom by horizontal strips. This can be found in the painted iron chamber clocks from Germany which were similar and which in turn followed the pattern shown in illustrations of Italian monastic alarm clocks. The Italian version seems to have stood on a bracket, with a crank to shake the alarum bell and a solid base instead of the lower horizontal bar. In Germany there was no base but the back upright had a loop by which it was hung on the wall with a crossbar for steadying. The alternative form of alarm was a second verge escapement working a double ended hammer inside the bell. It is best to be rather wary of this type: some of them have been attributed to the 14th Century, but they may still have been produced at the end of the 17th. They were normally of metal. The wooden ones were produced up to the end of the 19th Century, but are now being reproduced. These are more imaginative reproductions, analogous to the 20th Century water clock with 17th and 18th Century dates engraved on them.

In the true frame clocks the vertical bars run between upper and lower members which are united by pillars, and these upper and lower components may be rings, solid or skeletonised plates, or one of each. The construction and the method of assembly can give a clue to both date and provenance. In the commonest type of 'Gothic' clock there are two rings, and these are usually square, but there is good reason to believe that they were also made in other shapes. In the square clock the corner pillars are set at an angle and two slots are cut in the inner edge to take the rings. The lower edge of the lower slot is cut at an angle and the lower edge of the upper slot is undercut to form a square hook. The pillars are first hooked over the bottom ring, then brought upwards to meet the top ring, which is forced down to hold the pillars in place. The ring itself is secured by wedges along the top. The front and back vertical bars for the train are fixed to the rings which also support a bar carrying the centre upright. This type of construction was probably used in 1430, and is known to have been in use in 1460, but since it was still being employed in 1625 it can only give a very rough guide to the date. About 1580 the method was changed slightly and the pillars were fixed to the rings by rivets or screws. As the popularity of these clocks was on the wane it is unlikely that this practice lasted for more than about sixty years.

In the Gothic clocks the two trains were fitted one behind the other with the going train in front. Quarter striking work, where fitted, appears between the other two. In all but the latest of these clocks the striking is let off by a pin on the great wheel. Before condemning one with a star wheel under the dial it is worth examining the great wheel for signs of an original pin as many were 'modernised'. Iron is used exclusively in these clocks, which are mostly of Germanic origin. A further guide to dating lies in the decoration of the corner pillars: the more elaborate it is, the earlier the clock is likely to be. Again this is only a rough indication, as a maker would tend to keep to the style he had learnt in his youth and an overlap is to be expected. The elaborated pillar is exceptionally rare after 1590, and the simpler style seems to have come in about 1570. One further point to be noted is the way in which the weight actually drives the clock, whether it is passed over a pulley or fixed to a barrel. The pulley is the later version, appearing about 1500, while the barrel is indicated in the 14th Century clock-making manuscripts.

The automaton lion clocks all operate in the same way no matter how the lion may be standing. The eyes are connected to the balance and the lower jaw to the striking. As the clock ticks the eyes move from side to side, as it strikes the mouth opens and shuts.

(£120–1,200, $330–3,350)

The barrel was divided into two with the cord for the weight in one part and the winding cord in the other. As the weight dropped the winding cord was drawn up, and was then pulled down again to turn the barrel in the opposite direction and rewind the mechanism. Although few clocks survive with this device, traces of it can often be seen in those now fitted with a pulley. If the arbors seem to be inordinately long it can be a sign that there was once a barrel. Not all the barrels had a restraining clip like the pulleys, so there may be no sign of a groove in the arbor where this could have been fitted.

The late 17th Century basket-topped case may or may not be pierced. Most of the clocks of this period are by relatively well known makers and price depends to a great extent on condition and the state of the movement. A fair average price: £750, $2,100.

The evolution from the Gothic to the lantern clock is not yet completely clear, but it seems that first the upper ring was replaced by a skeletonised plate, then by a solid one, and then the lower ring too became a plate. The next change was in the corner pillars. These were slotted onto the corners of the plates and held by rivets or pins. As the pillars were riveted through holes in the plate the feet and finials either disappeared or were screwed to a thread on the pillar ends. In some cases they were dispensed with and nuts used. Although this is the apparent chronological order there is no clear cut division to simplify the dating of the various types, some of which remained standard in certain areas over many years while others too recurred. The lantern clock is a typical case. The iron prototype, complete with doors, can be seen in miniatures of the mid-16th Century, but the classical brass form with turned corner pillars does not seem to have developed until about 1630. Even then the slotted pillar was not abandoned but continued in use until at least 1700. It can be found in England, but usually in provincial clocks. After about this date lantern movements with square or arch dials were fitted in increasing numbers into long cases to become 30 hour grandfather clocks. The movement was no longer visible and the turned pillars were abandoned for plain ones of rectangular section; these were riveted to the top and bottom plates, and in some districts there was a return to iron frames.

From the front this clock would resemble some of the French clocks made in the late 17th Century. However the movement betrays its Dutch origin. Note the cycloidal cheeks on the pendulum suspension and the separate alarum movement in the top left-hand corner. Both details would add a premium to the price.
(£400–750, $1,100–2,100)

In England the frame construction was almost completely discontinued for domestic use before the end of the 18th Century. It was revived again in the early 20th Century when reproductions were made, and there is some evidence that the lantern was again in construction in the first part of the 19th Century for home consumption as well as for export to Turkey. Certain Continental types survived until the present century: the price of some is beginning to rise, but this is mainly due to the tourist trade and unscrupulous dealing and they are best left alone by the beginner.

Most of the frame clocks had trains fitted one behind the other, but examples do occur with the trains laid out side by side or with quarter and hour trains flanking the going trains but facing outwards. The most significant variant has the dial and count wheel at right angles to the train. This layout can be traced from the beginning of the 15th Century to the end of the 17th. As far as is known at present the idea originated in Burgundy and was only applied to clocks of French, Southern Dutch or North-west Italian manufacture. Any clock, weight or spring driven, with this characteristic should be acquired and put to the closest scrutiny to determine its age and nationality. Because the importance of these clocks has only recently been appreciated they have largely escaped the faker's hand and, at the most, they may have been embellished in an effort to give them greater interest. More often they are semi-derelict. With one important exception, all of these clocks so far discovered have iron movements.

The spring driven clock had been invented before the middle of the 15th

The bell-top case with the break-arch dial is probably the most common of all. They can be found in black, walnut or lacquer: mahogany is rare and so is marquetry, tortoiseshell and the more exotic woods. This type of case was being made practically throughout the 18th Century with a variety of movements. Even as late as 1956 a straightforward furnishing clock of this kind could be bought for £20, $56, today that price can be multiplied by four or five at least. This particular one is not typical, the dial is not usually in the arch and the supporting figure is most un-English.

Century; but the introduction of the new source of power brought a problem. The verge escapement is susceptible to variations in power and, as a spring exerts more force the more tightly it is wound, some method of equalising its output is needed. As far as we know, the first spring clock was a modification of the ordinary frame clock. The spring was coiled in a cylindrical drum which was mounted underneath the base. The end of the cord which had previously been fitted to the weight was fixed to the drum and the cord wound round it. The spring was pre-wound slightly to provide enough power to take all the cord off the barrel. The clock was wound in the usual way by turning the barrel, the motion being transferred to the spring by the cord. To overcome the varying power of the spring the barrel was tapered. This device ensures that the spring, when fully wound, acts on the smallest radius, which gradually

The larger clock, about 20″ high, is worth considering as an investment even at £600, $,1680. The price would be higher for a walnut case, this one is yew.

increases as the spring runs down and its power lessens. The conical barrel is known as a fusee, while the term barrel itself is applied in this type of clock to the drum containing the spring.

The initial method of construction with the spring below the base continued in use until about the end of the 16th Century, so that the collector may still be able to find an example of this type for a reasonable price, probably for no more than he would for one of the later form with the barrels above the

Another clock that needs the casemaker's attention. A basket top on a walnut case is not common nor are the cherub ornaments on the door. In general a walnut case will fetch a slightly higher price than ebony. A basket top will also enhance the value. The two together could mean an extra £100, $280 at least.

base plate. It is extremely unlikely that an open framed spring clock will be found today, as before the end of the 15th Century the movement came to be concealed in a decorative case made usually of gilt-metal. The frame form was still used inside these cases, but the ends of the corner pillars passed through the plates and were fastened either by a pin or by a nut. Although the frame construction was to continue for spring driven clocks until about 1700, its use was confined to Germany and Italy. The true ancestor of the modern clock, and, incidentally, the watch, had been produced by about 1460. Instead of running between narrow bars the wheels were set in two plates joined by pillars. The balance was arranged to move in a plane parallel to the plates by introducing a contrate wheel to drive the crown wheel through a right angle. The early examples of these plated clocks are almost invariably round, and the height is nearly equal to the diameter. The cases are gilt, drum-shaped, and have the dial at one end and a push-on lid at the other. At first no striking train was fitted, but an alarum attachment was made to stand on a tripod over the dial. The hand released the alarum through a trigger mechanism. All drum clocks are similar externally, apart

This type of clock is unusual for its date of about 1730 and the price does not seem to have risen to the extent that other types have done. About five years ago such a clock could have been bought for £500, $1,650 even though it is musical and relatively small, about 12″ high. Today it might still be bought for under £1,000, $2,800.

from the form of the dial—the 12 hour dial is almost exclusively French. The small door in the case opposite the fusee, showing when the clock needs to be wound, has also been claimed as a French characteristic, but is in fact no guarantee of nationality. Naturally, if the clock has a maker's mark this can provide proof of both provenance and date. Even if the mark is unidentifiable its position will give a clue. Roughly speaking, clocks made west of the Rhine are marked on the underside of the case, others on the back of the movement. But the main indication of nationality can be found in the actual construction of the movement. For some reason, the Germans pivoted the fusee and barrel between the plates, but not the wheels. These run between the front plate and arms fixed to the pillars with the crown wheel in a C-shaped clip also attached to one of the pillars. The back plate is usually skeletonised. Most drum clocks in existence are undoubtedly German, but it is worth examining any one of this type on the chance of finding an unexpected French example. Although the striking train usually appears between the same plates as the going work, frame practice did carry over into the plated construction in some clocks where it was mounted underneath. The bell was then mounted below the dial. These clocks are quite rare and mostly of late German origin. The French and Flemish makers carried over their 90° practice. Their clocks of this type have a vertical dial showing through a hole in the case, and this arrangement seems to have been imported into England. Some of them are found built on a square plan, but most are hexagonal. In these clocks the drive for the dial is taken off at a right angle from a pinion mounted below the great wheel. Exceptionally the two trains are completely separate with two plates in the centre. A few of these clocks may be found with iron plates and pillars: these seem to originate from the South-Eastern part of France, around Lyons and Aix-en-Provence.

The price of Knibb clocks has been rising steadily since the publication of R. A. Lee's book and they are beginning to challenge Tompion for high prices. When in doubt always seek expert advice as the price can vary greatly for reasons not apparent to the novice and at over £5,500, $15,500 only the rich can afford to take chances.

This type of 'pendule d'officier' shows the association with the later carriage clock better than the more ornate ones although it will not fetch such a high price. They were made about 1780.

(£250–450, $700–1,260)

The novelty of the ordinary clock began to wear off by the middle of the 16th Century: a few makers worked towards better timekeeping, but the general trend was towards more decoration or greater complexity, which involved either more dials, or the virtual transformation of clocks into toys by the addition of music or moving figures. Now as then, the price depends more on the complexity of the clock and the state of the case than on the technicalities of the movement. The astrolabic dial is probably the most sought after. The gearing necessary for these dials had been worked out centuries before, and it is hard to say why they were revived and included in domestic clocks. The widespread interest in astronomy was probably responsible, though it is equally possible that the purpose was astrological. At least one purely astrological clock is known. Whatever the reason, it is rare for the astrolabe dial to be unaccompanied; there are usually subsidiary dials showing the age, phase and aspect of the moon, the position of the sun and moon in the zodiac, the Italian and Nuremberg hours, the day, the month and the date. With all this extra mechanism to be driven, these clocks tended to keep even worse time than before, and they can hardly have been considered as serious scientific instruments so much as intellectual status symbols or presents for foreign dignitaries. They are expensive now, as they were then, but as few ever appear on the market, they are a good investment

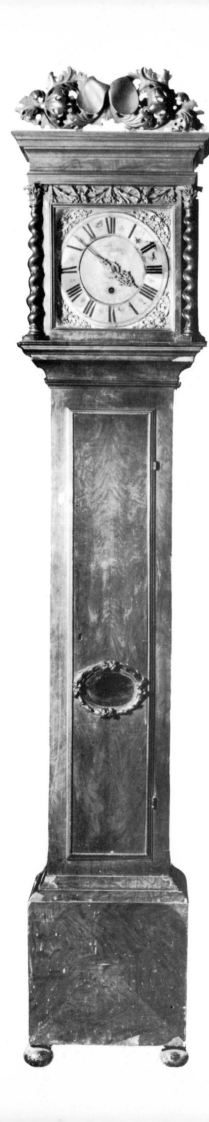

Left

This is a fine example of the early long-case clock but not necessarily fitted with a long pendulum. Even ten years ago such a clock would probably fetch £1,500, $4,200. Today that figure could easily be multiplied by three.

A good example of the nearly English clock. The carving of the cresting, the frieze above the dial and round the lunette in the door betrays the Dutch origin. The single winding-hole and the small disc in the centre of the show that this is an alarum-timepiece. The condition of the case is not good enough to push the price up but not bad enough to put it beyond the capabilities of a patient amateur. About three or four years ago such a clock might be picked up for anything between £30, $84 and £80, $225. Today the lowest price would be nearer the upper figure and is still worth paying.

Opposite

A late 18th Century watch and fob. The fob is possibly a little later than the watch. The sky on the back of the watch is of translucent pink enamel over an engine-turned ground giving the effect of sunlight. No paillons are used in the decoration for the case but they are used effectively on the fob, which is particularly fine and unusually complete. By and large enamelled fobs are less common than châtelaines.
(£120–300, $340-850)

This is almost more of a toy than a watch. A belt-buckle containing a watch for the Chinese market. These formed a large part of the stock of James Cox. The ornaments at either side of the buckle revolve, so does the decoration round the dial. This type of watch is quite rare and sought after.
(£300–1,000, $840-2,800)

An unusual type of decoration. The border and centre are decorated with coloured gold and set with pearls. There is a small diamond in the centre. The main decoration is built up in layers. The base is covered with flux to hold the small silver foil crosses, those are covered with a blue glaze and the remainder of the paillons and the white enamel is then fired on and glazed over.
(£80–160, $250-500)

This type of stone set watch may have been destined for export by the East India Company. There are slight variations in the outlines of the various cases also in the amount of enamel included in the decoration. Some watches have an agate plaque covering the back of the movement.
(£850–2,000, $2,400-5,600)

This is an uncommon variety of enamel. The green enamel in the scrollwork is straightforward champlevé but the bird and the flowers are built up and stand above the surface. This type of work was done in the second half of the 18th Century. Some were made in Geneva but most are Swedish. The raised enamel is liable to damage and few undamaged examples are to be found. Because they seldom appear on the market they have not become popular and considering their rarity are relatively cheap and can be bought for less than £100, $280 when they can be found.

In the words of the saleroom this watch is 'pavé' with pearls and emeralds. This type of decoration requires a lot of work, the pearls and emeralds have to be graded and the settings made up and fitted to the case; different settings are used for the pearls and the emeralds. The mixture of pearls and emeralds is unusual.

(£60–300, $170–850)

The winding button seen at the top of the pendant indicates a keyless watch. The decision to be made is, has a new movement been fitted? This does make some difference to the price. Quite a few small watches of the late 18th and 19th Century had keyless movements fitted in the beginning of the 20th Century to give them a new lease of life.

It is very difficult to date this watch on the appearance of the case. It could be about 1875 or 1925. The choice of dates would depend on the style of the movement, while the price will depend to some extent on the quality of the stones. Today's price would be at least £300, $900. As this watch has a relatively high intrinsic value it is a safe rather than a speculative investment.

There can be little doubt that the watch and châtelaine belong together. Ignoring the portrait, for the moment, the backgrounds agree both in colour and decoration, this includes the alternating use of red and blue as a background for the portraits and white dots as frames. As with any portrait watch some of the value will depend on the subject. In this instance no prizes are offered for correct identification but there are not always so many clues. No comparative price can be given as this is probably a unique specimen. It is equally impossible to give a reliable estimate of today's price but it would be surprising if if were under £2,000, $5,600.

An early 18th Century watch and châtelaine of the kind usually associated with Cabrier but used by other makers as well. This type has already been noted but here the price could be a little depressed by the absence of the original seal. The likelihood of finding a replacement is so small that it can be ignored.

This is the 'Pendule d'Officier' of about 1780. Although these are largely considered as being decorative clocks some of the movements too have interesting technical details. It is rare to find them still in their original carrying cases but it can happen. They have never been particularly cheap considering their size. Today a good one will fetch over £500, $1,400. Always examine the case and movement carefully as reproductions were made later.

for anyone who can afford them. Others will have to be content with the 19th Century electrotype copies. The really complex automaton and musical clocks have practically disappeared from the market, so that the price of the simpler models has started rising above the £1,000 mark. Nearly all these complicated clocks were made in central and Southern Germany.

Soon after the middle of the 17th Century the pendulum was successfully applied to clockwork, and, although the verge escapement was still used, timekeeping was much improved. In England, France and Holland, spring driven plated movements were standard. In this form the movement stands on edge, and the trains were arranged to bring the verge to the top centre with a short pendulum fitted instead of a balance. Many lantern clocks and other weight driven frame types were made with pendulums, and by now the wheel had turned full circle and the plated clock now became weight driven. The fusee in the plated clock was reformed into a barrel so that it could still be wound with a key through the dial. The case was extended downwards to protect the weight and the true long-case or grandfather clock was born. Before the end of the century the invention of a new escapement made the use of longer pendulums more practical, and the resulting time-keeping is still quite acceptable today. Most clocks dating from after the third quarter of the 17th Century are bought for practical rather than intel-

lectual reasons. Use and visual appeal become more important than academic interest. It is from this point that the whole basis of valuation for investment changes: although the demand for mechanically interesting clocks still exists, greater emphasis is put on maker and nationality. Famous makers may be expected to have produced better clocks—a fact which is reflected in the price—but an inferior clock with a name will often fetch more than a better one by an unknown maker. As the buyer becomes more expert in judging the quality of a clock he may be prepared to gamble on a maker who is either unknown or unfashionable.

Animals are always popular and these French clocks have good movements as befits such a setting. The prices have kept in step with French furniture in general. Prices rise almost from week to week and the easiest way to keep track of them is through Connaissance des Arts which has a section devoted to the salerooms and quotes prices.

The question of nationality does not apply to the French ormolu clocks where, particularly in the more exuberant specimens, the time telling function has shrunk almost to vanishing point. At the moment their appeal is practically universal, but as it is debatable how much of this is due to fashion, and they are far from cheap, it may be as well to leave them alone. In any case they should be treated as ornaments rather than clocks. This applies equally to the German clocks made a century earlier. They have steadily appreciated over the years and might be considered as a really long term investment for the benefit of grandchildren, but care must be taken to obtain them from a thoroughly reliable source. Both complete ormolu and ormolu mounted clocks have been reproduced in various qualities, and apart from these there are the late Victorian gilt clocks that are so fashionable today.

It is difficult to see this market continuing indefinitely. They were produced at minimum cost to sell as cheaply as possible, and although at first the movement did not suffer too much the cases were never good; they were made of zinc alloy and can be detected by their lightness and rough finish. Shortly after the middle of the 18th Century the increase in trade to the Near and Far East produced clocks which, though many were sold at home, were specially designed for export. These were made in England, France and Switzerland and are usually rather vulgar by present standards. They are confections more than constructions with automata and jewelled whirligigs moving to music played on bells or pipes. Sometimes they can be bought for under four figures if they are out of order, but this is a gamble. Unless the buyer can do his own restoration the repair bill can swallow any possible

Another French clock of the 1780's. The price will depend almost entirely on the quality of the metalwork and all the horological knowledge in the world will not help in establishing a price. If you find one in good condition going for £200, $560, buy it.

profit: if he does have the skill to do his own work he will, except where he is lucky, find himself in for a long job but at least is likely to make a profit on his outlay. If he calculates the value of his labour it will become apparent why these repairs are not done for shillings.

Towards the end of the 18th Century and in the beginning of the 19th a few French makers started producing high grade precision clocks which in their movements and cases have all the inherent beauty of good, functional mechanical design. Evidence shows that they were intended to have an international appeal, which they have retained. Although they are rarely cheap, they are sometimes not as expensive as they should be, usually because some finer point in their construction has been overlooked. It may be

The scientific interests of the 18th Century were reflected in the more functional clocks in which the movement was left open. In fact the indications are quite usual except for the one below the arch, this shows the four seasons of the year.

(£60–200, $168–560)

profitable to examine any of these clocks that occur, as this is a field where specialized knowledge can pay dividends. This knowledge can, to some extent, be obtained from the French technical books written between 1770 and 1830.

Except for the lucky find, few clocks can be bought today for much under £25, $70 and most of these were made in the last century. Is there then any chance for the man with little money? Probably. Several types are now selling for as many pounds as the shillings they cost a decade ago, and this represents more than just a reasonable return. Naturally the next question is, which to buy? It is impossible to see into the future, but it is likely to be the mixture as before. On one side the predominantly decorative, for example the individually made Art Nouveau clocks, on the other the mechanically interesting and then, as always, the novelty. The decorative clock is a very long term investment and not horological. The mechanically interesting: many of the non-synchronous electrical clocks have a relatively short working life and will soon disappear if they have not already done so. The novel:

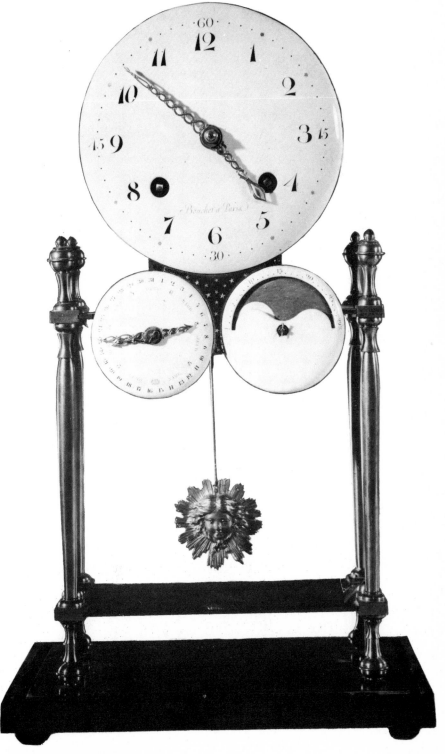

This clock was probably made after 1800 rather than before and the appeal is more functional than artistic.

(£40-150, $112-420)

the same applies. The collector of unconsidered trifles may get a very fair return. Novelty is also taken to include early prototypes. Has anyone an original Ingersoll alarm clock? But it will take ten or fifteen years for anything to appreciate, so this is a young man's field. With experience based on an intelligent study of patent specifications and trade journals of the last hundred years, he is unlikely to lose money in the long run and will probably earn the thanks of future horologists for preserving early specimens which would otherwise have been lost.

The Turkish market clocks are rarely as gaudy as those for the Orient, and are more in the English tradition. This one has a painted rather than a lacquered case with glass pillars. It has a musical movement with a choice of four tunes. The painted decoration on the dial plate is uncommon today. Ten years ago such a clock might be sold for less than £100, $280. Today you could treble that and still be too low.

Late 17th century cases with inlaid decoration are never cheap. The majority have movements by the better known makers and will fetch £3,000, $8,400 at least. The more famous the maker the higher the price.

This late 17th Century clock has a walnut case and shows that the earlier architectural style lingered on after the ebonised finish had gone out of fashion. Some purists might object to the width of the case but such a clock would cost over £2,000, $5,600 today having at least trebled in price in ten years.

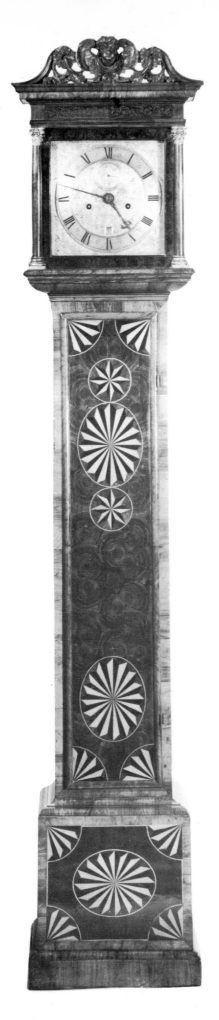

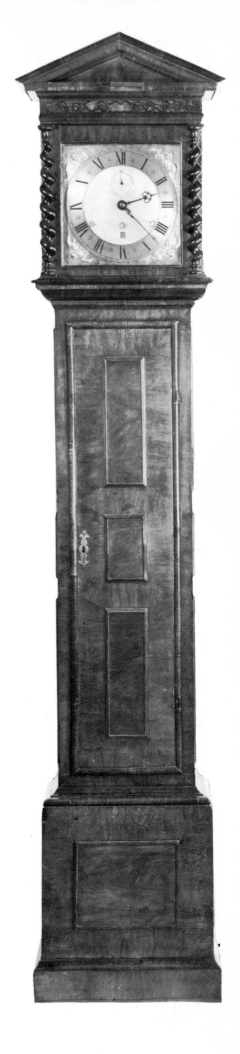

61

THE
DEVELOPMENT
OF THE WATCH

Once the spring-driven plated clock had been invented, the step to the watch was only a question of miniaturisation. The first watch was probably produced before the end of the 15th Century, in spite of the legend of the ' Nuremberg Egg ' and the claims made for Peter Henlein. It is impossible to be certain about the shape of the first specimens, but they were probably flattened versions of the drum clock, with the rare spherical watch the earliest variation. The few surviving watches of the spherical type can be dated near 1550—in fact one French example carries the date 1551.

There is in general more interest in the movements of early watches than in clocks, but this centres usually on appearance rather than technique except in one point, the stackfreed. This was a German device used, like the fusee,

in an attempt to compensate for the change in the force of the spring as it unwound. In the earliest stackfreed watches, the spring was open, and the outer end fixed to one of the pillars of the movement. A small pinion fitted over the winding square drove a wheel which was pivoted on the back plate. Two or three teeth on this wheel were left uncut, and by this restriction on its rotation the spring was prevented either from running down completely or from being too fully wound. The wheel also carried a cam which received pressure from a small roller attached to one end of a second spring. The other end of this spring was mounted on the back plate. The cams themselves can be found in various shapes, and there are several theories of why and how the stackfreed works. Today its main effect is to raise the price.

It is difficult, perhaps impossible, to present a simple picture of the evolution of the watch since there is at present no satisfactory system of classification. Nor has the significance of the various technical differences been fully evaluated, and, as the period from 1550 to 1650 has been the most popular with the fakers, the problem is yet further increased by the need to distinguish false from genuine. However, apart from the use of the stackfreed, which is almost exclusively German, there are no great technical variations between the watches of different countries up to the beginning of the last quarter of the 17th Century. The general rules for dials apply as much to watches as to clocks. The many shapes and varied decoration of watches of this period probably account for the attention which has been given to them by people otherwise uninterested in horology, and the various methods of case construction and decoration may provide a convenient way of breaking them down into groups. In most instances the arbitrary date 1650 will have to be ignored as technical changes rarely influence the outer appearance.

Virtually all the surviving early watches are in gilt-metal cases. A few are made up from sheet metal with engraved decoration after the drum clock practice, but a press-on lid is fitted to protect the hand, and pierced to make it visible. After about 1540 the lid hinged. Most of the piercing follows a geometric pattern, but by 1550 a design incorporating a series of holes, one for each hour, came into use. The holes are cut in the shape of a comma, the tail of one coming under the body of the next. The hand never disappears from sight as it does in the cast metal cases. Although a few cast tambour cases were made to contain ordinary watches, most hold clock watches, or at least have alarm mechanisms. The plain movements are pressed in from the back against a fixed dial but the striking or alarm types are attached to the dial which, together with the lid, is now hinged to the band of the case close to the pendant. The bell is screwed to the inside of the back of the case, which is now pierced. The piercing was at first confined to the band, but later spread to the back: by 1600 the band had become curved instead of straight and the pierced back became standard. It must be emphasized

Left

This is a connoisseur's watch and its true value could easily be overlooked. It is a crystal cased clock watch and the bell is hidden under the dial. This idea was used by Nicolaus Rugendus for quarter striking watches but not with crystal cases. This dates from about 1625. Ten years ago such a watch would probably bring £400, $1,150. Today those figures could be multiplied by at least four, possibly by as much as six. The movement could have a fusee or a stackfreed, which would affect the price.

Right

The regular octagonal form is allied to the round cased watch: both have circular movements. The long octagon has a movement of the same shape which is pushed into the case from the back. Most but not all are clock watches. The bell is very shallow and is screwed to the hinged back. They all have stackfreed movements with, as a rule, brass plates, although a very few can be found in steel. They are much less popular than the larger stackfreed watches but this may change as stackfreeds in general become more scarce. There is no good reason for the lower price as they are far less common than the other shapes.
(£100–600, $280–1,700)

This early 17th Century table clock could be English, French or Flemish but is very unlikely to be German. The bell for the striking is contained in the pierced dome under the dial. The decoration on the side of the case points to an English origin.
(£400–1,500, $1,100–4,500)

that the pierced back is found only when a bell is fitted, as there would otherwise be no protection for the movement. A pierced case housing an ordinary movement is always suspect. The round case was already being challenged by other shapes before 1600; first by the oval and later by the regular and long octagon. After the turn of the century a great variety of fantasy cases appeared, some still in metal, some in rock crystal and some in a mixture of both, while the use of enamel spread from the dial to the case. At first it was used only as an embellishment to the design, but then was extended to cover both inside and outside, initially in monochrome, later as new techniques were evolved, in polychrome pictures.

By 1700 the enamel case had almost disappeared and fashion had turned in favour of the relatively plain watch, which for technical reasons had become thick again. Better watchmakers were aiming at a thinner or smaller watch, preferably a combination of the two, and at the same time for greater precision and better timekeeping. Although the plain case persisted, there was a return to decoration with repoussé and cast forms, the continuing use of leather and tortoiseshell, with or without pin work, and of gold and silver inlay. The introduction of repeating mechanisms extended the life of the pierced case until the bell was replaced by the wire gong. For a while enamelling was confined to inset plaques of rather poor quality, but the full enamelled case gradually came back, often with a matching fob or chatelaine. It was extensively used on watches for the eastern market, many being made in exotic shapes. Very few rock crystal cases were made during the 18th Century, but blood-stone and striated agate were used for inserted plaques as well as for complete cases.

The turn of the century brought another change which had little initial effect on the external appearance of the watch. Several factories had previously started and failed, while batch and series production, which had been going on since about 1580 in a small way, was considerably extended by 1700. But the products were unfinished movements or ébauches, and were made by out-workers. The first factories tried to produce the complete watch under one roof—difficult in an age without tools capable of turning out interchangeable or even semi-finished parts using unskilled labour. They failed, while the ébauche trade continued on a far greater scale. The drive was towards a cheaper watch with mass production its inevitable culmination. Yet the 19th century was also an age of invention, with many patents granted for practicable and impracticable ideas. Some of both kinds reached production to provide material for the future collector and for today's investor.

Top left

An oval calendar watch of about 1620. The case is of gilt-metal, the covers silver. Most of these watches are French. The twenty-four hour dial is uncommon. The dial shows the hour, the date, and the age and phase of the moon, the day of the week appears in the lower aperture, the month in the upper. Like all early watches it is an investment.

(£450–1,000, $1,250–3,000)

Top right

Although most of the early watches with complicated dials were made in Europe some were made by emigrant craftsmen in Persia and Turkey. This is such a watch. Most cases are silver. The movement is often decorated with finely engraved complex scrollwork. These watches were still being made at the end of the 17th Century, after a continuous period of about sixty years. Sometimes these watches are worked over in an attempt to destroy their Oriental associations but this only succeeds in making them look like fakes. The price will depend greatly on the decoration of the case and the state of the movement.

(£400–1,000, $1,000–2,800)

Bottom left

The round, lobed crystal case is rarer and more attractive than the octagon. These watches date from about 1630–40 and usually have attractive movements. Many crystal cases were made in Geneva. Because of their rarity the price can be higher than that of some of the 17th Century enamels.

£1,000–2,000, $2,800–5,750)

Bottom right

A silver cased watch of about 1630. The glass was held in place by four wire clips passing through the bezel. Most of these cast silver cases have a floral design.

(£80–240, $220–700)

This brief review has ignored the finer points and the regional differences in the cases, quite apart from the movements, but it is impossible to give a simple yet accurate account of their evolution. This situation has led many collectors to specialize, but even then classification is very difficult unless the speciality is the work of one maker or one particular type of watch made by a selected group of makers. The system of classification by construction cannot be applied to watches as to clocks, except in their details, as until the second half of the 18th Century they were all fitted with plated movements.

The only possible system of grouping seems at the moment to be by shape: at first sight this appears to be too much like the old and unsatisfactory method of identifying clocks by external form. But the idea has some merit. The basic shapes to be found in watch cases are relatively few, but there are enough to make the initial divisions. To some extent the shapes are linked to periods, which will break the groups down further to manageable proportions, and the final identifications can be based on technical differences. The importance of the various sub-classifications will alter according to the period. This is hardly a final solution, but will be enough for the present purpose, especially if the materials of the cases are also taken into account.

The first round watches were the tambour type and were modifications of the drum clock. Most, perhaps all, originated in Germany and had steel stackfreed movements. They were largely clock watches or alarums. In this form the movement is clipped rather than pinned to the dial, which is itself hinged to the case together with the lid. The shape first began to change in the last quarter of the 16th Century, when the lid and the band became rounded and the mouldings on the edge of the lid and base disappeared. Castings were still used, but the design was lighter. The band was occasionally skeletonized and filled with a pierced and engraved panel of cast silver. The stackfreed was still used but steel gave way to brass, apparently for prestige rather than technical reasons. Some movements only appear to be of brass; the less easily visible front plate may still be of steel. Watches of this type have been known to fetch around £2,000, and since they have been forged in the past it is as well to look closely at them. Some are outright fakes, others have been made up from old and new material. No 16th Century watch is likely to have survived in perfect condition, and made up specimens are difficult to detect, all the more so since a number of originals were over-enthusiastically restored in the middle of the last century. The watch that looks too good for its supposed age should be distrusted immediately. The sharp edges and high points of the design would have lost their gilding. This might not be particularly noticeable in some of the earlier examples, as the

The dial is anachronistic for this type. This could mean that the movement has been modernised, probably with a new balance cock and a balance spring; possibly the whole escapement has been replaced. If most of the original movement still remains such a watch would be expected to sell for about £500, $1,400.

An early 17th Century crucifix watch also called a ' Montre d'Abbesse '. Virtually all the surviving cases are silver although gold ones are known. The more decoration there is on the case and dial the greater the price. This kind of watch was never cheap and in consequence does not show a particularly high yield but they are well above the vagaries of fashion and are safe, as are all early watches. It is quite possible that today's price is under estimated as there is no record of a recent sale.

(£450–900, $1,250–3,000)

A typical English dial of the mid-17th Century. This type of watch is rarely found in a gold case.

(£70–250, $190–700)

The chapters are not always placed radially. This type was popular about 1670. Any unusual arrangement of the dial will raise the price, as will the existence of a date ring, seen here. The difference due to a dial of this kind would be about £60, $170.

(£125–350, $350–750)

alloy is light in colour, but it can be detected by a difference in texture. The genuine movement will show signs of wear, with rebushed holes and perhaps later wheels and pinions. A balance spring may even have been fitted, and the stackfreed removed, leaving obvious holes. Although it takes experience to tell the over-restored steel movement from the fake, differences will appear. Luckily few fakers are completely familiar with the period and their work is flimsy and stilted. Typical mistakes are Gothic instead of Renaissance ornament, pins instead of catches, and screws instead of pins. In brass movements, steel was used for springs and arbors, occasionally for wheels on the back of the plate, and for the count-wheel, a ring toothed on its inner circumference which runs in a circular groove. Forgeries tend to have too much iron work which is too coarse and heavy. Broken and incomplete cases on these early watches have often been restored with electrotype copies made either from parts of the original case or from an entirely different one. Electrotyping was a commercial project before the start of large scale forging. In the electrotype process a cast of the object to be copied is coated with a thin layer of graphite on to which a skin of copper is deposited electrolytically. Then, in the old method, a reinforcing layer of zinc was added and the copy removed from the mould to be cleaned and gold plated on the outside. For the lid, moulds had to be made of both outside and inside: the two separate parts were soldered together before they were plated. The high quality of the finished article can be seen from some of the electrotypes on display in museums. The plating process tends to cover up the joints, and copies can most easily be detected by ear: they sound duller when tapped than the solid metal originals.

In the English and Dutch round watches of this period the band is not

An engraved, cast silver case circa 1640. It probably contains an English watch, and the value could be increased by removing the later shutter over the winding aperture even without plugging the holes. The condition of these watches is most important and they are still undervalued. It is surprising that the silver collectors have not taken them up.

(£100–250, $270–700)

Strangely the lack of a calendar ring will be more than compensated for by the existence of an outer case and given a good maker the price today can go as high as £450, $1,250 against the £350, $750 quoted elsewhere. This only goes to show that there can be no hard and fast rules in investing.

The six hour dial is a collector's item. With the extra space between the chapters and the faster revolution of the hand it was possible to get a closer estimation of the time. The minute scale surrounds the chapter ring. These are sometimes mistakenly called 'Italian dials'. The pendant and ring of this particular watch are about 100 years later than the watch itself: this would have an effect on the price. The figure quoted applies to a watch by an 'ordinary' maker and would be higher for one by a famous name, particularly Quare or Tompion.

(£100–150, $200–300)

The hinge on the outer case is not only square but has a slight undercut which could indicate a Continental origin, the piercing and long pendant point to a repeating watch in which case Quare's name would add to the price, although not so much as Tompion's. The watch appears to be in good condition with a plain bezel round the dial. These cases are normally plain except for the piercing.

(£100–250, $250–850)

usually curved, but retains the mouldings that were originally part of the lid and base. The covers may be of silver, with possibly a silver overlay round the centre of the band. The later types tend to lose the mouldings and the band is slightly rounded with an almost elliptical section so that its curved edges blend into the lid and back. English watches can very often be identified by an engraved border round the back plate of the movement, but this was also a Flemish practice and is not exclusive. However, most watches other than those readily identifiable as Germanic are inscribed with the name of the maker.

Oval watches made between 1590 and 1640 present the same problems of identification. There is still no difficulty with the Germanic type, since those that are unsigned follow the old pattern, particularly in keeping the stackfreed, but there was a return to the older method of sliding the movement into the case from the back and fastening it with latches. The small round dial which is usually overlaid in silver and decorated with basse-taille enamel is integral with the rather pointed oval case. The dimensions are relatively small for a clock watch—about 2 inches is the normal length. The back opens and carries the round, slightly domed bell. At this time the stackfreed remained but brass was used for the movement and the annular count-wheel was sometimes replaced by a disc fitted on the front of the movement to be visible through a heart shaped hole in the case. The specific point of origin of this oval type has not yet been found, but it can be easily identified by the lack of any decoration on the exterior except some moulding on the band and, in later examples, some simple engraving. This plainness may have been caused by the influence of the Reformed Church, just as in England the 'Puritan' watch was produced—a small plain timepiece in silver or gold that is more nearly egg shaped than any other kind. There is no band, and the back blends into the line of the lid, which has a circular glazed opening. There are also plain oval French watches, but these keep the band and there is no applied chapter-ring on the dial: the numerals are engraved directly on to the plate. The movement was pushed into the case from the front and secured by two spring bolts released by small knobs on the dial. The hinged movement really belongs to the decorated type which has the lid and back of engraved silver and an applied silver band.

Not all the German watches were fitted with stackfreeds, some large clock watches with fusees in the going train at least can be found in oval cases: the bell was shaped to fit the case, and was sometimes placed under the dial so that the case front had to be domed and pierced. The oval clock watches are fairly large and heavy, and many were mounted on circular bases with turned pillars so as to become small clocks.

At the beginning of the 17th Century the fantasy or form watches developed, with cases shaped as stars, crucifixes, skulls, birds, animals, shells and flower buds. Some were made partly or wholly of rock crystal or less commonly of some other stone. Occasionally enamel was used to embellish the engraved decoration of the mounts or the complete case. Most were signed, so that their nationality is easy to establish. They are generally French or English although some were made in Geneva. The movements are technically uninteresting and so much alike as to raise suspicions of a common origin despite the signatures. This does not, however, have any real effect on the high prices that these watches fetch. Because of their delicacy they were often supplied with protective outer cases to guard them from damage when lying in jewel boxes. These covers came to be used to protect the watch from every-day wear, and this led to the decoration of the outer case and the growth of the pair-cased watch. The octagonal types, either long or regular, are very similar to the ovals and show the same differences according to their nationality. During the 17th Century the form watch, and later the oval, died out and the round form gradually became standard. A flatter movement was introduced, and while the diameter varied greatly the height remained fairly constant. Again the movements themselves show a curious similarity which even extends to the decorative copperplate style of the signature. A thorough comparative study may reveal a common origin and provide evidence of an early attempt at mass production. This would not imply the use of interchangeable components which appeared only after the invention of better machinery.

During the last quarter of the 17th Century the balance spring was invented and had the same significance to the watch as the pendulum had to the clock. Its immediate effect was to produce a thicker watch. Previously this had tended to become flatter and generally smaller in diameter, and the balance had rarely occupied more than an eighth of the backplate area. A balance as small as this would have needed a weak spring too delicate to be made by existing techniques. This led to a larger and heavier balance. The greater power necessary was supplied by widening the mainspring as well as thickening it, and it was this that increased the depth of the movement. In the earlier watches without balance springs the balance had been carried in a cock which was first pinned to a tenon on the backplate and later fixed by a screw. The decoration had also progressed. What had been a functional C-shape or a spiral had become the main decorative feature of the backplate and was now pierced and engraved with floral motifs, while the foot fixed to the plate was at least as large as the table which covered the balance. With the

Top left
This type of crystal case should not be confused with those of the early 17th Century. This watch was made in Vienna at the end of the 19th Century. The design of the bow is typical. Note the style of enamelling on the bezel and the general appearance of the dial. For many years these watches were looked down on although they are enamelled on silver. These were the years after it had been shown that they were not 17th century. At that time they could be picked up for £10, $30, although they held the old inflated price in some hopeful shops. Today the price is creeping up again and a good example will fetch £100, $350.

Top right
An un-typical Blois dial of about 1650–60. The centre of the dial is usually plain blue. This is champlevé enamel, the floral spray in the centre is the metal of the base and not applied. The case is champlevé. As this is not a typical watch a figure of £750, $2,200 is only an estimate of today's price.

Centre
This is another of the problematic association watches. Traditionally the initials on the back of the case are those of Mary, Queen of Scots. But the maker is Pierre Duhamel who was working in Blois, Geneva and Paris in the third quarter of the 17th Century. There might be another maker with the same name but the dial and outer case agree with the known Duhamel. In addition, the initials may be read as M.P.C. Horologically it is of little importance but it would make a great difference to the price.

Bottom left
There is a great deal of apparent difference between the watch at top left and this one but they are both products of the same town at the same period, and there would be little difference in the price.

Bottom right
The portrait is supposed to be that of Madame de Maintenon, mistress of Louis XIV whose portrait appears on the inside of the case. The movement is signed Jacques Soret of whom nothing is known. However, there is another watch with the same signature which has a balance spring and so it can be assumed that he was working about 1680. The case is of a type attributed to Pierre Huaud, the father, who died in 1680 but who left no signed examples of his work. As Madame de Maintenon died in 1684 the association is quite possible and could be verified by comparison with existing portraits of both herself and Louis XIV. The decoration is most important, the blue of the ground is typical of Blois, and the work around the case is flat for all practical purposes although the white stands a little proud in places. The monochrome pictures are produced by laying the same colour with differing densities. The portrait is straightforward painting but with some stippling for the shading of the flesh. Close examination of the miniature shows that the dark background was laid on and fired last. Today an ordinary watch attributable to the father of the Huauds would probably fetch over £1,500, $4,500. Who knows what effect the other associations would have on the price?

Top

An early 17th Century example of a pierced watchcase with applied enamel decoration resembling the earlier Renaissance jewellery. The dial, which can be seen through the cover, is of course later.

This is a more elaborate version of the preceding type and should not be confused with the painted, floral enamels. The enamel is applied to a pierced gold design mounted over an inner, enamelled case.

Centre

This case shows an interesting variation of the champlevé technique. The surface is prepared in the usual way but the ground is matted with a ring punch instead of being filled with enamel. The white enamel for the leaves and petals is applied in blobs and fired. The colour is then applied and the case refired.

The inside of the lid and the dial are straightforward champlevé enamels. The cast case is engraved and heightened with solid, white enamel.

At first sight this might be confused with champlevé enamel but it is known as ' émail-en-resille-sur-verre '. As yet there is no alternative name. The ground is of blue glass and is hollow. The enamel is contained in gold fired into the glass. It is probable that this type of enamel was designed to be mounted over either silver foil or silvered metal which would tend to make the background seem luminous. No attempt can be made to estimate the prices of any of these five watches might fetch. They are included as comparative examples in case such watches should appear on the market.

Bottom

A good example of guilloche enamel. This is also included to show a minor variation in technique. The ground decoration is produced on a lathe, the flowers are engraved by hand.

The border decoration on this case is of coloured gold. The central scene is a return to the early basse-taille technique. The variation in the tone of the blue enamel is produced by cutting the ground to a greater depth where a darker shade is required. Thus, although the surface is completely smooth and may be polished, the depth of the enamel is not the same throughout.

(£25–95, $70–270)

larger balance the foot was made much smaller and the metal thickened to provide the strength needed. The French abolished the single-footed cock and used a bridge with a screw at either end. This could accommodate a balance almost as large as the backplate. The decorated circular table was retained, but now had two small ears to take the screws. In French and Swiss watches these changes meant that the position of the winding square had to be altered, and they were wound from the front either through a hole in the dial or through the centre of the single hand. The Dutch and English balances were rarely large enough to interfere with the winding and when they were they were redesigned so that the arms moved clear of the square, which now passed through the balance and the cock. This method was also sometimes used in Switzerland. Even when the balance became smaller again the French, Swiss and some Dutch makers kept the bridge, although in Geneva some watches were still produced mainly for export with balance cocks ' à l'anglaise '. The larger watch naturally brought about changes in case design which can be divided roughly to agree with the use of the cock or the bridge. Some watches ' à l'anglaise ' were produced with single cases, but the tendency was towards pair cases, and the remainder, perhaps because they were wound through the dial, retained the single case. They came to be known as ' oignons ' because of their high domed glasses which were fitted into the upper edge of an almost vertical bezel. It is very likely that they originally had protective cases, but these are rarely found. Most ' oignons ' are of gilt metal with slightly raised decoration though plain cases are found in both gilt metal and silver and a few have survived with gold cases. The classic dial for this type is of gilt metal with the hour numerals on separate enamel plaques set round an enamel ring which carries the quarter divisions. After the introduction of the concentric minute hand a further ring was added outside the chapters with small plaques for each fifth minute. Blue enamel on a white ground is usual, but black is sometimes found on Swiss dials. In addition to the cartouche dial there are two fully enamelled kinds, one plain white with large black chapters and another with numerals painted on bosses which were raised on the blank before enamelling. The bosses are often outlined to resemble cartouches. There seems to be no chronological division between the three types and by 1700 they had all started to give way to the metal champlevé dial and later to a more simple white enamel form.

There are naturally exceptions to the rules which associate cocks and bridges with particular cases. Many pair-cased watches are found with bridges: some are either Dutch or Swiss but the majority are claimed as English. Their exact origin is still a subject for research. They are often referred to as ' Dutch fakes ' although the latest evidence suggests that the movements were fitted to silver pair-cases in the Netherlands and were imported from somewhere else. The dials of these watches usually have the minute scale formed as a series of arches, but similar dials were also made in Geneva. The main point of identification is the balance bridge which has pronounced asymmetrical feet rather than symmetrical ears. They were mostly housed in silver pair-cases with repoussé decoration on the outer.

Except for a few isolated examples the single case had died out in England and Holland by 1700 but the true pair-case does not seem to have come into use immediately and the outer case was still covered with leather or tortoiseshell. Either might be decorated with abstract designs or initials in pin work but the shell often had armorial bearings or inlaid pictorial decoration in gold or silver. The outer case of the true pair-cased watch is always of the same metal as the inner and was originally plain. During the 18th Century the amount of decoration gradually increased although the plain style was never completely abandoned. The piercing of clock watches and alarums was extended to the outer case but as the clearly defined band had disappeared it took the form either of a frieze or of small panels. This pattern was retained for repeaters, which slowly replaced clock watches after about 1680. The repeating watch struck the last hour and quarter only when required, and the mechanism was operated by pressing the pendant. The half quarter repeater was a further development where the double blows indicating the quarter could be followed by a further single stroke. At about the same date the concentric minute hand came into general use, as a consequence perhaps of the improved standard of timekeeping which had accompanied the introduction

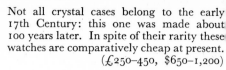

Not all crystal cases belong to the early 17th Century: this one was made about 100 years later. In spite of their rarity these watches are comparatively cheap at present.
(£250–450, $650–1,200)

A gold repoussé-cased watch of about 1720. The subject of the decoration is not the usual mythological scene. For this reason the price would probably be rather above the norm today as buyers are becoming more discerning. This was not so much the case ten years ago, so the price rise would be somewhat greater. The symmetrical scrollwork in the frame is also an attractive feature. A casemaker's mark or signature would probably influence the price, and a premium would also be paid for a movement by one of the famous names. The condition of this case is very good which accounts for the slightly high quotation. The inner case would be undecorated.
(£50–250, $150–750)

Cases with coloured gold decoration sometimes set with turquoises or garnets are still reasonable but condition is important as little can be done to restore worn specimens. Obviously a really good example would fetch a higher price.
(£25–60, $70–200)

A case of this kind may be of Continental origin but can be found on an English watch of about 1730. The pierced case indicates a repeating watch. The condition is not really good and this would affect the price.
(£50–120, $150–350)

A repoussé gold pair-cased watch of about 1750–60. The style is Continental rather than English. The subject is taken from classical mythology and is therefore somewhat less interesting to the specialist collectors. The scrollwork of the frame incorporates architectural features. A few of these cases may be cast rather than repoussé. The growth rate of this kind of case will probably increase as collectors become more numerous.
(£30–100, $90–300)

of the balance spring and now made the extra hand something more than a novelty. Alternatively a six hour dial was sometimes used: since the hour hand moved twice as fast and the spaces between the chapters were twice as large the hours could be divided into twelve and the time read to the nearest $2\frac{1}{2}$ minutes with relative ease. In the chronoscope or wandering hour watch a semi-circular slot was cut in the upper part of the dial revealing a disc which revolved once in two hours. Two apertures on the dial, one showing the odd hours and the other the even, indicated the minutes as they passed a scale on the top edge of the slot. The sun and moon dial was another application of the same idea, where an ordinary minute hand was provided and the hours were again marked on a semi-circular opening on the dial and

This case only looks as if it is repoussé, actually it is cast silver and signed 'Cochin' the maker of these cases in the 1740–1760 period. They stand up to wear better than the repoussé variety and although it is rare to find them in mint condition good examples can still be bought quite cheaply.
(£3–20, $10–70)

A repoussé allegorical scene on a gold pair-cased watch of about 1735. The chain by the pendant is to hold the outer case while the watch is being wound. The four small cartouches round the main scene on the back of the case contain surveying instruments and other items connected with astronomy, timekeeping and navigation; these would have a great effect on the price. The case would probably be signed and contain a watch by a well known maker. Ten years ago it might have been possible to buy a watch for as little as £250, $700. Today it will be more likely to fetch £750–1,000 and might go as high as $3,000 in America. The appreciation and identification of unusual decoration can pay dividends.

The plain agate cases are much cheaper than those set with precious stones but they are worth buying if in good condition.
(£70–150, $200–450)

Although this type of agate case is less showy than others it compensates for its lack of precious stones by the fineness of the technique. These were produced by a method similar to that used for small cameos; a suitably large piece of striated agate had to be found and cut to leave the dark striations standing against a translucent background.
(£750–1,500, $2,200–5,000)

A repeating watch in gold pair-cases, about 1710–20. The condition is excellent and would make a large difference to the price. The piercing indicative of a clock watch or repeater can be seen round the side of the case. This type of case will fetch a higher price than that fitted to a plain watch as the inner case is also pierced and engraved. A watch of this kind in silver would fetch about a third of the price of a gold one. This is largely because few silver cases are to be found in really good condition. Most buyers have overlooked the fact that certain designs and patterns were made in silver only.
(£90–500, $150–1,750)

indicated by representations of the sun and moon on a disc revolving in 24 hours. Nearly all the dials were metal, but soon after 1700 there was a return to the enamel dial, and there is no definite evidence that this had ever completely died out since its first use in conjunction with enamelled cases.

All the essentials of the modern watch were brought into being and at least partly perfected during the 18th and early 19th Centuries: although the precision machinery needed for cheap mass production had still to be developed, the first successful factories were operating before 1800. All this has led to another collecting interest which centres on the technical details of the movement rather than the artistic merits of the cases. The successful investor in this field needs specialised technical knowledge which is not easily acquired. To most collectors little of technical or artistic interest was produced after 1830, but more attention is now being given to the later period, especially in America where collections are being built up of high grade and complicated 19th and 20th Century watches in addition to the products of the American factories. Very little has been done in this area in Europe, except in the field of high grade watches, and as a result prices are still low.

In the first part of the 18th Century the plain case was sometimes engraved, but the most common form of decoration incorporated a design produced by raising the metal. In the early examples the effect is fairly restrained, but most show classical scenes enclosed in symmetrical or asymmetrical scroll work. At times the metal around the chief figures was cut away to leave them free standing, and the background was filled with an engraved plate. In the second half of the century enamel decoration was revived and, as the repoussé style died out, cases of coloured gold came in together with those

machine engraved on a rose-engine. At the same time a cheaper grade of silver pair-cased watch was produced as well as the gilt metal type. The silver was confined to the inner case and the mounts of the outer, which was covered in tortoiseshell. The darker variety was used mainly for exported watches or for the deeper cases. The lighter was made more interesting by underpainting. After the tortoiseshell had been moulded to fit the case it could be decorated in two ways. If there were well defined dark patches the painting aimed at a reproduction of moss agate although multicoloured butterflies were sometimes added. Clear shell was treated more ambitiously, possibly as an imitation of enamel, and the centre of the back was filled with a miniature in either an oval or a vesica shape. This style is often incorrectly called *vernis martin*, which properly applies to a much rarer type of pictorial decoration in coloured varnish sometimes used to produce imitation tortoiseshell. As collectors have so far ignored the under-painted shell case and many have been broken up for the silver content, good specimens are becoming rare.

The watch with the classical champlevé dial has been creeping up the price scale. Those in silver have only just really started moving. The maker's name and the type of watch will make a difference. For a 'named' repeater, £200–650, $560–1,800.

This is a relatively plain version of the 'Chronoscope'. The minutes are indicated by the position of the aperture in which the hour appears.

(£150–500, $420–1,400)

The 'chronoscope' is a variation of the standard dial. Some can be found that were made before 1700. The square hinge of the outer case is an indication of the early date. The design in the lower half of the dial varies, some have engraved decoration instead of the repoussé work seen here. Sometimes there is a portrait medallion of the reigning Sovereign, and naturally these will fetch a higher price.

(£150–500, $420–1,500)

Watches for the Turkish market were produced in great numbers. Some remained in stock for many years and passed straight into collections. For this reason 'Turkish' watches can be found in completely mint condition. Obviously the price depends too much on condition to give any sensible estimate. All that can be said is that the finest specimens could be bought for about £10, $30, less than a relatively poor example will fetch today. A Turkish silver outer protecting case in addition to the usual triple silver cases can add to the price.

A mid-18th Century export watch. The striated agate panels are set in a repoussé gold frame decorated with diamond set floral sprays.

(£350–500, $900–1,500)

THE
ENAMELLED
WATCH

For collectors mainly interested in the external appearance of the watch the enamelled case holds pride of place. Watches with enamelled decoration were probably made in the early part of the 16th Century but none appear to have survived. From about 1580 the basse-taille dial was used in Germany with a rather formal foliate pattern in the centre and often with exotic looking birds. The material of the dial was silver and the chapters and design were deeply engraved to take the enamel—opaque black or blue for the numerals, coloured and transparent for the ornament. On the best dials the metal was suitably engraved where it would be visible through the enamel. Primary colours were used, although variations in tone can be found. Unfortunately the silver was not of high quality and the impurities have tended to loosen the enamel with age: complete examples are thus moderately rare except where the whole dial was covered with a transparent flux. A few gold basse-taille cases have survived, but they date mostly from the early 17th Century. A still rarer version of basse-taille has free-standing gold foliage applied to a plain gold case, with the leaves and petals hollowed slightly to hold the enamel. A third variant, *émail-en-résille-sur-verre*, is almost legendary; hardly any watch cases can be found intact, although a few pieces of jewellery remain. This was a tedious process and was probably never used to any great extent. A thin gold sheet was cut to shape and formed into a shallow dome which was filled with wax. The design was impressed on the outside of the gold and the wax replaced with a blue translucent glass. The gold shell was then filed down revealing a blue surround to the impressed design, which was next filled with transparent enamel and fired. The enamel used had a low silica content so that it would flow before the glass melted. This is the simplest method, but other more complex processes were known. A mixture of calcium, lead and tin, known as calx, could be added to the enamel to make it opaque,

This is one for the experts. The bezel may or may not be a replacement, some bezels were enamelled in the same style as the case. The assessment of this will depend greatly on the colours used. There is a clue to the origin of this case in the butterfly below and between the numerals XI and XII: this could point to a German provenance and the case might well have been made in the third quarter of the 17th Century rather than the second. These cases are actually rarer than those made in France but they have not appreciated to the same extent.

(£350–750, $1,000–2,500)

Even with all the pearls and pastes this type of guillochée enamelled case tends towards a lower price than those with a less encumbered back. They date from about 1820 or a little later. The common colour is blue.

(£50–100, $140–280)

The back of this watch is decorated with transparent enamel over a ' guillochée ' or engine turned ground. This technique was used for about a decade on either side of 1800. Dark blue and red were the most commonly applied colours. A variety of movements can be found in these cases and will naturally affect the price but they are less expensive than the painted enamels.

(£280–550, $780–1,600)

It is almost impossible to evaluate this type of watch without close examination. These early 19th Century enamel cases may contain plain watches or musical quarter repeaters with or without automata. The price can double between the two extremes. The quality of the painting and the condition of the case also have to be considered.

(£350–850, $1,000–2,500 for
an average example)

The design on the back is typical of those produced in Fleurier for the Chinese market, but these cases contain a variety of movements, some with names of English makers who may have imported the enamel plaques. These are fitted into the back bezel in the same way as a glass. Many of these cases are silver, some are silver-gilt and a few are gold. The Fleurier watches were usually sold in pairs and a pair will fetch more than two single items, especially if they are still in their original tortoiseshell-covered box. The price varies according to the movement and the metal of the case. The figure here is for gold.

(£120–200, $350–600)

Another form of the Fleurier enamel watch-back. This one has a bouquet of flowers against a background of guilloché enamel. The usual consideration has to be given to the case and movement but as a general rule the price tends to decrease as the flowers get smaller. Gilt metal cases can occur with this type of bezel and are relatively cheap.

(£20–45, $50–150)

Another watch which needs research to achieve its value. The gold case is decorated with coloured gold and has an enamel plaque set into the back. At first sight there is just a balloon sailing over a landscape but comparison with contemporary prints indicates the possibility that this is the flight of the first hydrogen balloon, between the Tuileries and Nesle in 1783. Research of this kind can increase the price of a watch by 50% or more. This watch was bought for £30, $184 and sold for £130, $364.

Small, early 19th century pendant watches can almost be considered as costume jewellery, the visible, gem-set balance is an asset. The dial is the most decorative feature, the back is often plain.

(£100–300, $500–1,750)

and solid enamel was used on cases either to build up a design out of blobs of various shapes, which were sometimes heightened in a contrasting colour, or by covering a gold or copper shell inside and out to produce a case that appeared to be entirely of enamel. This second technique was used extensively in Blois, and both types sometimes incorporated settings for precious or semi-precious stones. The blue cases characteristic of Blois were rarely plain, but had a fairly simple design in black or white. Occasionally a landscape is sketched in black on the inside. Most of these fully enamelled examples had covers over the dial which matched the body of the case, and the movement was fitted with an enamel dial, with black roman numerals on a white ring. The centre of the dial also usually matched the case except when raised enamel had been used. The Limoges method of pictorial enamelling does not seem to have been applied to watch cases. There are one or two watches with what appear to be Limoges enamel plaques in the lid and back, but they seem to belong to the 17th Century and may be even later.

The early technique of enamelling used previously prepared coloured enamels which were crushed to a fine powder, laid on to the ground and fired. The colours themselves were largely produced by the addition of metallic oxides in different proportions. In the first part of the 17th Century a new method was discovered which produced a very different result known today as 'painted enamel'. A white enamel base was fired on to the gold or copper shell and decorated with the oxides previously used for making the coloured enamels. After the painting was complete the case was fired again. As the oxides and the metal of the shell were separated by the white base there was no danger of reaction and a greater range of colours and tones could be used. In the early examples much of the white is visible and the colours are quite soft: they became more solid in the middle of the century, but never harsh and brilliant as they did after about 1670.

So far there has been no comprehensive study of the enamelled watch. The early cases, and indeed the discovery of the process, are credited to the Toutin family: although it is unlikely that they had no apprentices their own distinctive style was sharply divided from that of the Huauds of Geneva. This difference, which is largely one of technique, is all the more surprising as there was a considerable overlap in their working dates. Jean Toutin had worked at Blois and Châteaudun and came to Paris about 1632 where he was joined by his eldest son Henri. Jean died in 1644, but Henri lived until at least 1683. The younger Jean, Henri's brother, went to Sweden in 1645 as enameller to Queen Christina and died about 1660. Pierre Huaud came from Chatellerault to Geneva in 1630 to finish his apprenticeship. He is known to have been an enameller as he himself had an apprentice in 1661

Top

A gold and enamel cased watch of the late 18th Century, made for the Turkish market. Few of this type have been offered for sale so far.

(£180, $500)

The artist has produced what he imagines to be a Turkish seascape. Both the shape of the miniature and the surrounding scroll-work are indicative of a better quality watch. These have not yet become really popular.

(£350, $900)

Centre

The segmented case has enamel decoration alternating with applied coloured gold.

(£180–650, $840–1,820)

The back of the case has been carelessly replaced and shows that these backs are separate productions. The quality of the work is not particularly high and could occur on a silver case. In silver the price would be about £80–90, $224–250.

Bottom

This is a gold and enamel cased watch of about 1800 and was probably sold in Constantinople by Le Roy. The enamelled bow shows that it is of better quality than usual and this will be reflected in the movement. Some of these have been going relatively cheaply lately.

(£350, $900)

A Turkish watch of this quality could legitimately have Breguet's name on it. In some instances it might have a fully developed Breguet movement but it is more usual to find a good Swiss movement finished in the Breguet workshop. Even with Breguet's name such a watch could be bought for about £500, $1,400.

to whom he agreed to teach *peinture sur émail*. Several cases are attributed to Pierre Huaud, but there is no known signed work. These cases show a combination of two techniques; the ground is blue with a portrait medallion in the centre, which is surrounded by four small landscapes sketched in red and enclosed in raised white borders of symmetrical scroll work. These frames are separated by a formal floral design also raised in white. Of all the decoration only the portrait is 'painted'. The elder Pierre was succeeded by three sons: Pierre, born in 1647, Jean-Pierre, in 1655, and Amy, in 1657.

The eldest son went to Germany for a year in 1685, returned there in 1689 to become painter to the Elector of Brandenburg in 1691 and died in about 1698. Jean-Pierre worked on his own for a time, but in 1682 he and his younger brother joined together to become 'Les Frères Huaud'. They too

Top left

One dial of a double-dialled watch for export to the Orient. The other dial would probably have centre-seconds. This dial indicates the date and age of the moon in addition to the time; the lower dial is to regulate the watch. The case is of gilt-metal and is set with coloured pastes. Most of these watches were made during the last quarter of the 18th Century and have only recently begun to appreciate. The maker's name has a direct bearing on the price. The watches signed by James Cox will fetch the highest prices.

(£60–180, $170–500)

Top right

A multi-dial watch showing the hours, minutes, full and fifth seconds and the date. In addition, and this is the important part, it has the magic name of James Cox. The gold case has inset agate panels. The number on the dial could possibly be the date but is more likely to be the serial number. Items by James Cox have been going up steadily and such a watch will fetch about £400, $2,250 today.

Bottom left

Multi-dial watches are usually a reasonable investment providing they have either some age or quality. This watch is old enough and has the added attraction of a visible balance. Starting from the top and moving in a clockwise direction the dials indicate hours, minutes, second, quarter-seconds; the next is for the regulator; the last is a lunar calendar. The price will depend on the case and movement but correct identification is important.

Bottom right

A clock-watch for the Chinese market. Gilt-metal case set with pastes and split pearls. The diameter can vary between 2″ and 6″ with a consequent variation in price. These watches can be double dialled and some have automata on the back which work in conjunction with a small carillon. The price will depend greatly on the condition of the movement.

(£70–200, $200–500)

went to Germany in 1686 and returned to Geneva in 1700. Jean-Pierre died in 1723 and Amy in 1729. The signature has several variations, and the name may appear as Huaud, Huaut or Huault. The last two forms are more common on work produced after their return to Switzerland. The productions of the Huaud school are quite distinctive. The colours are bright and rather hard. The main subject covers the back of the case and has a narrow yellow border, while the sides have small framed landscapes and a plaque with the signature opposite the pendant. The inside of the case is usually decorated with a landscape, but both the style and the colours are different. The inference is that each brother worked separately, and it is known that there were craftsmen who specialised in the inner decoration. Comparative research is hampered by the fact that few signed pieces exist apart from those of the Huaud brothers. Further complications are introduced by the migration of artists and the export of their work.

The fully enamelled case began to die out at the beginning of the 18th Century while the use of enamelled dials increased. The painted enamel was confined to small circular miniatures set into the back of the outer case or mounted on the balance bridge so that it was visible through a glazed opening in the back, an idea which originated before the end of the 17th Century.

A real automaton repeater. The two figures
actually strike a bell mounted under the
dial. £60–140, $170–480. But look for the
automaton on top of the column!

A more expensive version of the automaton
repeater. The gold putti have to climb the
pillars to reach the bells.
(£80–800 $230–2,300)

Singing bird watches are rare in any form.
This type is more spectacular than the one
in which the bird is concealed in the band
of the case. No exact comparative price is
possible. Today one would have to think in
terms of £3,000, $8,500 as a minimum
starting price. Condition must be taken
into consideration, especially on the mechanical side. Repairs to such a watch could
easily cost £500, $1,400.

An even more exotic version of the automaton repeater. The repeating part has
been consigned to the lower part of the plate,
even the dial itself might be considered to
be subsidiary to the main automaton,
' Moses striking the rock '. The background
to the scene is executed in enamel. When
the repeating action starts, Moses strikes
the rock and a shutter opens to reveal a
twisted glass rod rotating to simulate running water. This is probably the rarest of
all the automaton repeaters. No comparative figure is available but today's price
would be close to £2,000, $5,600.

Yet another version of the automaton repeater. In this one the automata consists
of the girl in the swing and the jet of water
emerging from the fountain.
(£120–600, $350–1,650)

These ' souvenir ' watches were made in
Vienna about 1780 by Johann Holtzmann.
They are not normally so elaborate in their
decoration. The movement of the watch is
contained in the lower case. This one is
unusual in that the decoration suggests that
it could have belonged to Louis XVI.
(£250–750, $700–2,100)

A more elaborate version of the automaton
repeater. While the two amorini strike their
bells the cutler at the bottom sharpens his
knife on a grindstone turned by his assistant.
(£120–600, $350–1,650)

85

This is the classical dial for the Oignon watches made in France and Switzerland just before 1700. The numerals are blue on French watches but black on the Swiss. The watch is wound through the centre of the hand. The enamel is on to the metal, separate plaques are only used for repairs. Condition is all important. Later examples have an outer ring of enamel for the minutes.

On the right watch this type of case can add £30, $84 at least, especially with the rose and crown. The decoration is silver laid in tortoiseshell. The date is about 1700. The silver is set in with heat and the larger areas are secured with rivets.

It is difficult to explain the decline of painted enamel. It may be due to the rise in popularity of the enamel dial for both clocks and watches, which must have provided plenty of work and an opportunity for greater profit with less demand on the skill of the artist. A more likely reason is perhaps the increase in the demand for enamelled boxes and other items. Portrait boxes can be traced back to before 1700, so there is some overlap; during the 18th Century the connection between the gold box makers and the watch case makers seems to have become increasingly close and it is quite possible that men of fashion ordered box, fob and watch as a set. Re-uniting these individual items could prove to be a profitable pastime—engraved and engine

It is rare to find a watch in a case like this although it can happen. This should not be confused with the form watch. The sounding board contains a small musical box. Price depends on condition and the number of diamonds: anything under £1,000, $2,800 is unlikely unless in very bad condition.

Watches with cases in the shape of musical instruments were popular in the early 19th Century. The cases are of gold with enamel decoration. The back of this violin opens to disclose the dial of a small verge watch. The price does not show a great increase as these forms of watches have been popular for many years now.

(£200–350, $550–1,000)

turned examples exist as well as those with enamel decoration. Practically every technique, form of decoration and even material used for snuff boxes were also used for watch cases, but here the only concern is with enamel either applied directly to the case or to portrait miniatures set into a frame on the back of the watch. The framed miniature had been used in silver cases, but the gold counterpart is a much finer form. The case itself was decorated with gold of a contrasting colour in a raised floral motif often heightened with enamel. The miniature was framed in paste or diamonds, as was the bezel, and often the frame formed part of a larger pattern of gems. The enamelled miniatures were probably bought from a factor. This system was later extended to the supply of complete watch backs, which were set into a bezel in the same way as the glass. Even where the enamelling was integral with the case it was usually the work of a specialist. The old type of fully enamelled case went out of favour and, indeed, was no longer a possibility with the pair case and the later single case which opened from

A difficult watch to evaluate. It is clearly
setting out to imitate the 17th Century case
in which the enamel decoration is on a gold
framework applied over a plain or more
often an enamelled ground. The question
is, when was it made? Allowing that it is
Viennese the pendant argues against the
probability of a late 19th Century date.
About 1780 is probable and this type of
watch at that date is exceedingly rare, so
rare that ten years ago the price would have
been adversely affected.

(£25–600, $70–1,700)

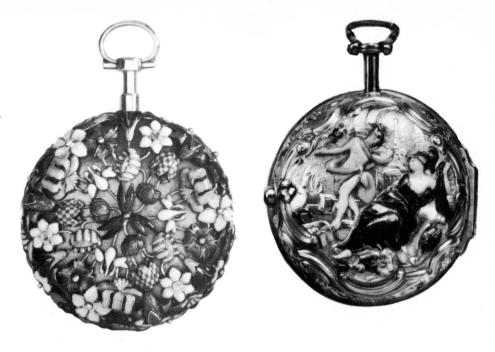

A rare combination of repoussé and enamel.
The two figures, Mercury and Britannia,
are enamelled in colour. The implications
of the whole scene might be worth investiga-
tion. The building in the background,
between the two figures might be the Pharos
at Alexandria. This type of case is much
rarer than its price would indicate.

(£70–160, $195–450)

The pearl and enamel border is unlikely on
a gilt-metal case but the central decoration
is not. Also the enamel on the gold cases
has a higher gloss and will wear better. The
fountain is made of applied, coloured gold
and the 'stones' may be pastes but diamonds
are more likely on a gold case. In gold
£75–200, $–210–560 in gilt-metal £5–25,
$14–70.

The central ornament is the balance wheel,
set with pastes or diamond chips and oscil-
lating against a background of blued steel.
Unless the watch is in good mechanical
order the full effect will be lost and the price
will suffer accordingly. The inclusion of set
stones in the picture is not to everyone's
taste nor is this particular use of paillons,
but the mechanical aspect will help the
price.

(£160–250, $450–750)

Although the pailloné enamel is good quality
it is not up to the so-called 'peacock's tail'.
However the under-cut glass decoration in
the centre is most unusual. Rare as it may
be it could be bought for about £100, $300
today.

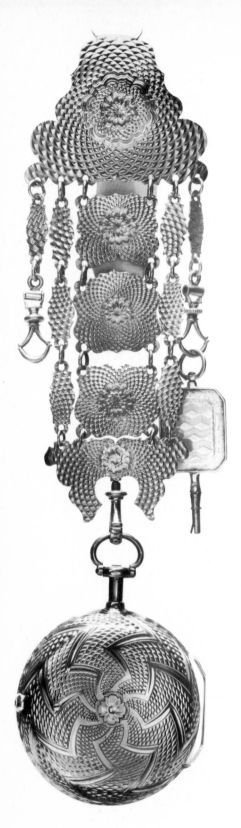

The 'Sun and Moon' dial usually has a concentric minute hand but some fly-back hands may be found. In these the minute hand only moves across the upper part of the dial and quickly returns to its starting point at the hour. The hour is indicated by the image of the sun or moon on the central disc. A good example by a well known maker would fetch £70–300, $196–840.

Opposite Top

This is a representative example of the so called portrait case of the late 18th Century. Whereas the earlier ones may have represented actual people the later miniatures are purely decorative. The floral sprays are in coloured gold and set against a matt background: the flowers are 'gem-set' to match the frame of the miniature. In this quality the 'gems' are more likely to be paste but may be roughly cut diamond chips.

(£20–60, $56–170)

The true portrait watches of the late 18th Century are rare. It is surprising that they have been overlooked by the collectors of miniatures. The portrait is of Marat and was probably done in Geneva as Jean Paul Marat was born near Neuchâtel. He was a friend of Abraham-Louis Breguet and it was Marat's laissez-passer that permitted Breguet to escape from France. It is impossible to give an accurate estimate for this kind of watch as too much depends on the interest aroused by the association. The wreath round the portrait is composed of gold and silver paillons.

The unusual is not always appreciated and this watch and châtelaine would not fetch as much as one with repoussé decoration. The two do not necessarily belong together but they are both produced by the same technique. Each large component of the châtelaine is cut from the centre of a plaque about the same size as the back of the watch. The links are made from the off-cuts. The spiral pattern is an optical illusion, it is actually made up of concentric, wavy circles.

Centre

This watch is similar to the one above but is a more elaborate production. The portrait has an integral border of green basse-taille enamel, diamonds are used for the outer frame and are set in the bow and top of the pendant. The coloured gold floral spray is partially enamelled. Strangely, all this makes less difference to the price than might be expected.

(£45–95, $140–300)

At first sight this is another watch of a type which has already been estimated but there are differences that could affect the future price. Firstly, the pearls of the bezel are flanked by twisted gold wire and secondly, the diamond-set rosette in the centre of the back has been decorated with enamel, at first sight these may seem like rubies. There is little doubt that the rosette is original as it fits in too well with the turned decoration. At the present time a price of £10–20, $30–60 would not be unreasonable.

In general this type of case is less common than the portrait miniature form. The enamel used tends to be on the soft side and scratches easily so that really good examples are difficult to find. It is customary to attribute this type of scene to the influence of Watteau for obvious reasons. The enamel is fired onto the case and the floral sprays round the engraved frame are of champlevé enamel. No real guide can be given to the price as too much depends on the condition of the enamel which can cause a variation of as much as £50, $150 between two watches in the same sale. The better one will detract from the value of the other.

Bottom

This type of enamel is almost typical of the poor quality enamels being produced at the end of the 18th Century and beginning of the 19th Century even on gold cases as here, the enamelling on the base metal case is even worse. Nevertheless they are part of the decorative history of the watch and advantage should be taken of the relatively low price. There is an interesting technical aspect to the enamelling: the back of the case has a series of concentric circles cut on it; these relieve the monotony of the translucent blue 'sky' but also act as a key for the painted enamel. The decoration incorporates paillons and set pastes. The tree is partly painted, partly paillonné.

(£25–60, $70–180)

This watch is most important. There are two aspects to it, one purely decorative, the other documentary. The white enamel ground carries the repoussé gold decoration which is decorated with translucent green enamel. The documentary importance lies in the fact that the case is signed ' GUIL-LAUME BOUVIER ' in the scrollwork. Bouvier, a member of a Genevan watch-making family, was working as an enameller in Paris about 1740. But the gold work has ' COCHIN F ' raised in the gold at the lower edge of the central group it figures. David Cochin was a repoussé worker in Geneva about 1730 who later moved to Paris. The importance of this watch lies in the fact that it underlines the co-operation between trades in the production of decorated watch cases. It is unlikely that the two men were working in the same shop. It is more probable that Bouvier bought the Cochin decoration. Here it is not possible to provide an accurate estimate as no one can say how important this watch may be to the collector.

Opposite

There may be some doubt that the châtelaine and the watch belong together, apart from the differences in subject and colouring. The scrollwork of the châtelaine is asymmetrical. No such doubt can be expressed in comparison between the back of the watch and the brooch. However, this possibility of marriage between watch and châtelaine would have little effect on today's price. If it did it would be more than compensated for by the presence of the brooch. This watch was made about 1780 and the decoration should be compared with the earlier Huaud case.

(£900–2,500, $2,550–7,000)

Painted enamel, paillons and pearls. The light colourlng may sometimes have an adverse affect on the price.

(£40–120, $112–350)

Three examples of cheap Genevan enamels of the late 18th century. These are gilt metal cases. Although a similar type of enamel can be found on gold cases they are exceptions. The enamel is usually fired onto the body of the case but some inserted backs are found. The quality of the paintings varies, some are poor, most are mediocre, a few are almost good. At the present time this type of watch rarely reaches £50, $140. In many instances these watches are sold as part of a lot rather than individually. Good examples are likely to appreciate as they form an essential part of the history of enamelling.

This page

The automata found on watches and boxes can exist separately, in pendants. There is the usual musical accompaniment.

(£300–950, $850–2,650)

At times the separate musical automata were made small enough to be fitted into a ring or brooch. Their rarity is offset by their size which makes them less impressive and tends to keep the price down. However there are signs that their rarity is being realised and the rate of appreciation may be accelerating.

(£200–750, $560–2,100)

The mid 18th Century agate case may have coloured gold, applied decoration. This may be badly rubbed and can depress the price rather than lifting it. A good example should go over £750, $2,100.

A calendar watch of about 1810 with painted decoration on the dial. The use of double ended hands is interesting but often overlooked. One hand shows the day of the week and the appropriate planetary sign. The other indicates the month and the sign of the zodiac. The visible balance is an added attraction. In a gold case £20–60, $56–170. In silver today's price would be about £15–20, $42–56.

the side almost along the centre line. The last vestiges of the band disappeared and the front and back of the case met a pair of moulded rings incorporating the hinge.

The nearest subsequent approach to the enamelled case can be found later in the products of Meissen, Bilston and other similar factories. In these the backs and fronts were set into the hinge rings with another ring in the front to take the glass. Normally they were enamelled on copper but porcelain ones are known. Another type of fully enamelled case was produced about 1740 without painted decoration. They have repoussé gold figures and scroll work fired onto a white ground. A method close to the old style of painting appears on what might be considered as enamelled versions of the repoussé case. A scene executed in enamel on the back is enclosed in an engraved or raised irregular border. The extension of this idea brought champlevé floral decoration in polychrome enamel although it is more common to find the basse-taille technique using a deep blue flux. The blue was also often applied over an engine turned ground, either completely covering the back or as a surround to a painted scene. Plain transparent enamel was often relieved by paillons, small pieces of coloured gold foil of various shapes forming a design and held in place by a clear glaze. Most of these were made up separately and set into the bezel with split pearls. Paillons were also used on the cheap enamelled gilt brass cases of the late 18th and 19th Centuries, but in conjunction with opaque colours. It is obviously impractical to describe all the different forms of enamel decoration to be found on watches up to about 1830, but two are worth noticing. Both were designed for export to countries outside Europe and are popularly divided into the Turkish and Chinese groups. Broadly, they originated respectively in England and Switzerland. The English continued to use a full plate movement in enamelled

gold triple cases. The inner was decorated with flowers or a trophy in a mixture champlevé and basse-taille, the back of the centre case had a land or seascape with a transparent pink enamel sky over engine turning representing sunrise while the outer was simply two decorated rings hinged together. The back had a glass to protect the enamel of the centre case. The resemblance of these enamels to others produced in Geneva suggests that many of the craftsmen working on this type of case had in fact emigrated from there.

This type of enamel decoration is often found on the gold cases of watches by Thomas Mudge. Matching châtelaines were also made. The enamel may be blue basse-taille or polychrome champlevé. As with all enamel watches the price depends on condition and polychrome decoration will bring the higher price. However this type of decoration has never really been favoured by collectors but it is showing signs of gaining ground.

(£100–175, $250–500)

The fully enamelled case of the late 17th Century is liable to damage at the pendant which will affect the price. The decoration is taken from the Old Testament and is less common than the classical scenes, it is probably the work of the Huaud family and may well have been done by the brothers Jean-Pierre and Amy when they were in Berlin.

(£450–1,250, $1,200–3,500)

An early pictorial enamelled case of about 1640 re-made a century later. This type of case is something to be watched for. Old cases were cut up and re-used but Guillaume Bouvier, an enameller who was working in Paris about 1740, closely followed the style of the earlier masters particularly the Toutins. To some extent the price would depend on the scene on the inside of the case.

(£450–1,250, $1,250–3,500)

Stone set watch cases of this kind are even rarer than the similar Neuber snuff boxes. Some cases were made in Dresden but they were also produced in Geneva. The basic framework is gold.

(£350–850, $950–2,400)

The 'Chinese' watch was different in every respect. The movement consisted of a front plate to which were fixed the dial and a cock carrying the back pivots of the wheels. The cocks were rectangular or had a complex serpentine outline. Both shapes were usually decorated with fine foliate scrollwork of champlevé engraving with the design standing out. Nearly all the movements had centre seconds and were fitted into the single case from the back. There was no hinged bezel and the watch was wound and set through holes in the cuvette or inner dome, which was often glazed to show the movement. Most of the cases are silver gilt—gold is exceptional. As the enamel is confined to the back, manufactured separately, the case proper consists only of a centre band with two bezels, integral at the front and hinged at the back. The bezels, the pendant and the bow were often set with split pearls, and the backs were decorated with a variety of designs, although floral patterns were the most popular.

The second wave of form watches were decorated almost exclusively with enamel. This time there were no stars and crucifixes and animals, but musical instruments were common. Practically the only shapes found in both periods are shells and buds. The enamelled watches made after about 1830 are rarely found either in public or in private collections. This lack of interest means that their price, when they do appear, is very modest, and, surprisingly, differs very little between those with blue or black champlevé work and the painted enamel types. The best of the period combine both of these with basse-taille technique. A small painting is surrounded by an engraved scroll border which itself stands out against a black background. The whole area is covered by a clear glaze, and the rest of the case is engraved. In the late 19th and early 20th Centuries enamel laid over engine turning reappeared.

This particular form of painting may be in full colour but it can be almost monochrome against a pink or blue background tint. Even when colours are used they tend to be very light in tone and resemble those of the latter half of the 18th Century. In general these later ones have not appreciated as much as they might have done.
(£350–500, $900–1,300)

A diamond set gold and enamel cased watch of about 1820. The possible royal association suggested by the initials do not affect the price as much as might be expected. Ten years ago it might have fetched about £100, $280. Today the price might have doubled.

A gold cased watch of about 1780. The back is set with an enamel portrait medallion which, if it could be identified, might make a great deal of difference to the price.
(£75–150, $200–400)

A straightforward silver cased calendar watch of the 1630s. These watches are sometimes found by English provincial makers who have been somewhat overlooked so far. They are well worth buying. They can still be found occasionally within this range but are overdue for a rise.
(£175–200, $500–600)

The usual colours are powder blue, pink and grey. Individual work was rarely done except under Art Nouveau influence, and so far only one or two examples of this type have come on the market and have been sold at ridiculously low prices.

At the end of the 18th Century more stringent navigational requirements led to a search for more accurate timekeeping, and the watches developed for this have attracted the attention of a group of collectors not only for the technical details of the movement but also for the simple elegance common to many of them. Most keep time to a standard well up to present day needs and are often carried to give pleasure to their fortunate owners throughout the day. In this field the maker's name counts for something, but not to the exclusion of the technicalities of the watch itself: an ordinary watch by a specialist maker rarely fetches more than one by any other. The one exception to this rule is A-L. Breguet. The main point of attraction is the escapement, with the lever and then the chronometer varieties exciting the most interest. The definitive history of this short period from 1780 to about 1825 is still being written, and the student is referred to the specialist works on the subject, particularly *Watches* by Clutton and Daniels.

The automaton and musical clocks had their counterparts among the watches. In the middle of the 18th Century the music was played on a nest of bells, but the number was limited by the space available and the tunes can at best be described as simple. Later when the bells were replaced by metal reeds the popular tunes of the day were used. There is no record of any music written specially for watches by known composers, as was the case with the larger mechanical instruments. The first of these watches contained a miniature version of the musical box with a pinned barrel and reeds set at right angles to the surface. The early ones are rare, but the same system was used in later and cheaper watches, especially the 19th Century musical alarms. The later examples can be identified by the pin barrel which can be seen lying across the movement, while one end only of the much smaller barrel is visible in the earlier ones. Most musical watches have the tune pinned onto both sides of a disc and the reeds screwed alternately to both sides of the front plate of the movement. In the bell and the reed types the music is usually played automatically every hour and a silencing lever is fitted to disconnect the lift from the mechanism. They can also be played at any time by pushing a slide. Closely allied to the musical watch but infinitely rarer is the singing bird watch. There are two types, and in one the bird appears from behind a hinged panel in the back of the watch. In the other it springs up through a slot in the back of the case opposite the pendant. As the bird moves while it is singing this variety comes into the automaton category. The simplest form of automaton is the repeater with two coloured gold figures either side of the dial which strike imitation bells when the hours and quarters are repeated. There are many variations on this theme. Amorini climbing pillars to strike bells, knights tilting in time with the blows, Father Time striking a bell with his scythe. In some, the figures strike real bells set under a raised dial. The pornographic automata are found mostly in repeating watches with striking figures. The scene is normally concealed by a panel below the dial, but ordinary repeaters were often modified at a later date to have the secret panel set in the inner dome. In both types the required motion is supplied by the repeating train. The longer run needed for the musical train provided the opportunity for constructing more complex automaton scenes, among them smithies, carpenters' shops, quarries, kitchens with flickering open fires, waterfalls, rivers and fountains and scenes with coloured gold figures moving against an enamelled background. The watches themselves, together with their automata, were fitted into snuff boxes, spy glasses, lorgnettes and scent sprays in the form of pistols. The French Revolution brought the production of these watches almost to a halt, with only a few being made for export. However, the main reason for the disappearance of the fantasy was the fact that customers with money to spend were turning to elegant precision watches while at the same time the financial gains offered by the expanding market for cheap watches tended to reduce the number of skilled craftsmen.

Opposite
Top

A Turkish market watch of about 1830–40. The scalloped edge to the case will probably lift the price a little.

(£40–130, $112–370)

Not all the Turkish Market watches had high grade enamelled decorations. This applies particularly to the early 19th Century period. However this applies to the colours of the enamels rather than the technique. These watches are still relatively cheap and will appreciate. This particular watch might reach a higher price as it is a repeater. This is indicated by the flat button on top of the pendant.

(£25–100, $70–280)

Centre

This gold cased repeating watch is of the late 19th Century or even early 20th. The repeating may be only the quarters but minutes are possible. Do not lose your head, the high-grade repeating watches do not have a push on the side of the case but a slide. The cases are usually very thin and flimsy. The diamond set decoration indicates the original destination of the watch and should set the price. Cost varies greatly but £40–60, $112–168 plus the value of the diamonds is fair but make sure that both the case and the movement are in good condition.

Bottom

The lack of enamel decoration would tend to keep the price down but here the value of the fob must be taken into consideration even though it is of an earlier period. The wise investor will separate the two keeping the fob for a pair or triple-cased watch.

(£60–175, $170–500)

A repeating watch of the second quarter of the 19th Century. The style of decoration could indicate an export watch. The condition will make a difference to the price and in conjunction with a fine movement the price would be doubled.

(£40–130, $112–370)

This page

A really late form watch, possibly as late as 1920. The late date is indicated by the position of the winding button. The earlier keyless models are wound at the head. As late as three years ago such a watch might be bought for under its break-up price, today £300, $840 upwards is more likely. Other decorative watches of this period are still cheap and should be sought out before they too start to rise in price.

CAVEAT

EMPTOR

In the financial world a wise man will investigate the company into which he intends to put his money. This is, or should be, elementary common sense but many people still get their fingers burnt. Few collectors, especially in the second half of the 19th Century and early years of the 20th century, were horological specialists and there was much indiscriminate and uninformed buying. Most people were looking for cabinet pieces and were only interested in showy externals. One dealer who was almost a wholesaler even went so

This is a real speculator's piece and ripe for skullduggery. As it stands it would fetch something over £200, $560 today. Obviously the case is French, probably made in the south rather than the north and more likely to be before 1600 than after. The upper band of the base is almost certainly a later addition. The movement does not belong. The temptation would be to case the movement, re-make the case and make a movement to fit.

The movement of this automaton clock is fitted in the base. The time is indicated by the ' Moor ' who points to a chapter ring on the rotating globe. When the hour is struck the figure turns its head and the dog at its feet leaps. Many have stackfreed movements in brass, they are German and were popular in the first half of the 17th Century.

(£150–850, $400–2,500)

far as to advise collectors to avoid plain watches, however good, and to concentrate on the decorative pieces. It is suspected that he did this partly to create a market for his ' beautifications ' and partly to be able to buy at a low price the plain watches which were the raw material of his trade. Tragic as was the absence of the horological specialist even more tragic was the lack of interest among art historians in the actual decoration of cases, so that many clocks and watches were accepted as genuine which embodied a strange mixture of periods and styles in their decoration. The trade did their best to cope with the demands of this booming market. They were not always too particular how they did it. In some instances there were honest attempts to restore derelict specimens but on the other hand many good clocks and watches were ruined by the unscrupulous few by ornamental additions aimed at improving the price rather than the article. This idea of embellishing seemingly uninteresting pieces was not, even then, a new idea in horology. Some examples can be traced back to the beginning of the 19th Century with certainty while a few date back to about 1780.

There was one good result of this indiscriminate buying. Many pieces were preserved which would otherwise have disappeared. The difficulty today is not always one of separating the wholly true from the wholly false but deciding how much may be original. It takes much longer to decide that an object is a fake than to declare it genuine—although there are those who will pronounce condemnation at the drop of a hat. Equally there are those who accept everything as genuine and this is what happened in the early part of the 20th Century when the historians started work. Naturally they assumed that the clocks and watches they were using to formulate their theories were correct, especially where the dealers had made some effort to provide a

In point of fact this is really neither a clock nor a watch. It is more of an elaborate watch-stand. The price will depend entirely on the quality of the porcelain and the ormolu mount. These clocks appear in porcelain sales and shops. It is rare to see them even thought of as furniture.

credible provenance. They were also hampered by the difficulties of communication which made visits to a large number of collections virtually impossible, the lack of comprehensive bibliographies, the absence of any comparative system due to an unscientific approach and lastly, their ignorance of the practical side of clock work. Even so, their work is not valueless. At least we can profit from their mistakes. Also the difficulty of travel forced them to make a more complete study of a particular area. This produced the many invaluable records which form the basis of much of today's research.

None the less, they did establish a traditional history which was accepted and followed uncritically by all but a few of their successors, producing many of the popular misconceptions which are still widely believed in spite of the efforts by the few to dispel them. Today there are perhaps twelve horological experts in the world, all more or less specialists in a particular field. Each one is prepared to admit to his limitations when and as the occasion arises. The future for the investor lies in the hands of these men. The word investor

With minor variations this type of case is the most common on clocks of the late 17th and early 18th Century. They are mostly black but walnut and some tortoiseshell are found. The size varies and the price with it. The smaller the case is, the higher the price will be. Clocks in these cases should be approached carefully. If they are all original they are as safe as houses but there have been many marriages between case and movement and more than a few have later cases. A similar looking clock was still being made in the 1920's. The price can range from £80, $224, to £10,000, $28,000 depending on what is inside and how big it is.

is used deliberately. The speculator may or may not suffer on a short term basis as he usually deals in the fashionable market. But these phases of speculation have been seen before and have passed leaving the last purchaser a sadder but wiser man.

How should the investor proceed? The pursuit of perfection is often unprofitable but much depends on the age of the piece concerned. Early 19th Century enamelled watches in mint condition can be found. Many of

Almost an equal mixture of clock and ornament. It is capable of telling the time and can be considered as a furnishing clock and is more likely to be sold as a clock than as an ornament. The price will vary with the quality but the price would run upward from £150, $450 and you could not expect anything very good for that money.

The plain walnut case of the first few years of the 18th Century does not fetch as high a price as one with inlay.

(£1,750, $5,000)

Floral marquetry should command a higher price than the geometrical inlay of the same period and even a little more than the more exuberant decoration of the 18th Century. The price has at least quadrupled in the last ten years, regardless of the maker. A good case alone can fetch £500, $1,400 if not more. Even at this price it is worth considering on the chance of finding a good contemporary movement.

these were originally bought as curios or for presentation rather than for everyday use and their initial high price ensured that they were well cared for. The further one goes back the less chance there is of finding anything in perfect condition and so the more suspect such a piece should become. But at the same time the price will soar. What the investor should be looking for is complete credibility rather than perfection but the buyer should guard against self-delusion. It hardly matters that he believes in what he has unless he can prove it conclusively to others. He must initially be sceptical but he should never be dogmatic.

Rectangular as opposed to square dials do occur with bell top cases and are usually by good makers. Even without close examination you can see that you would be buying work. It is unusual to find the movement in good condition if the case looks neglected. The later hands are not an encouraging sign. The lack of a dummy bob would mean that the original escapement has been replaced by an anchor. However if close examination shows that the movement and case were originally together and the works have not been completely gutted and given a name like Tompion a purchase price of £750, $2,100 would probably show a profit after restoration had been paid for.

If the prospect of successful horological investment looks black, it is a mistaken impression. It has never been so good. International communications are quick, photographs are relatively cheap and illustrated books abound. All this makes do-it-yourself research more of a practical proposition than it ever was. Additionally, most of the early horological confections have passed from the open market. This makes it almost impossible to obtain illustrations as they have been accepted as genuine more often than not.

With those that are still on the market the possibility of legal action arising from such illustrations deters people from using them so that detection remains a personal effort. This applies not only to antiques as such, but to the contemporary forgeries which were made for trade purposes. However, the position is now improving. Some museums have held exhibitions of fakes and there are some collectors today who are actively looking for such pieces. The word fake is used very loosely today to cover true fakes, over-enthusiastic restorations, forgeries, reproductions and, of course, those clocks and watches that are right in part and while almost coming under the heading of restorations are still fakes. The true fake sets out to deceive by pretending to an antiquity or a personal association that it does not possess. The clock or

A connoisseur's clock. It belongs to none of the common classifications, in consequence it could go for under the current price for the usual types. Say £750, $2,100 as against £1,500, $4,200. The clock might be Flemish but is more likely to be Dutch.

watch falling into this category may be a complete fabrication or a genuine antique to which has been added a maker's name, a coat-of-arms or an inscription. Forgeries were aimed at the contemporary market—a practice that is still with us. The reproduction was not intended to deceive anyone at the time it was made but became accepted by collectors who were only too ready to believe that they had made a find. There are recorded instances of reproductions sold by antique shops in good faith at ten times the current manufacturer's price, and this is still happening. To judge from the contents of many of the shops it always will.

With restorations the problem is more difficult. How much restoration is to be permitted before it can be considered as faking? If an unsigned clock

The double basket top does not always mean a high price. In any case they should be examined carefully for damage and/or replacement. The gilt-metal ornament round the door is correct with the type of top. Assuming that all the ornament is in good condition it should add £75–100, $210–280 to the estimated price.

All these enamelled gold form watches are early 19th Century productions. Many, if not all, were primarily designed for export to the Orient. A little over ten years ago £35, $100 would have bought any one of them, today they are past the £200, $560 mark. The decoration may vary slightly from one to another and this may make for slight variations in price. None of these particular forms has so far proved to be more valuable than another. They should not be thought of as serious watches. The movements are not of high quality and there is little to be gained from putting them in going order. Although the majority of these watches were made in the 1800s the three on the right are late 18th Century.

Left

An early 18th Century French bracket clock. The decoration is in brass and tortoiseshell, the dial is bronze with blue chapters on white enamel plaques.

(Wallace Collection)

A less common type of repoussé gold outer case. Note that the scrollwork of the frame is not quite symmetrical and the pillar separating the two figures is more decorative than practical. It is these apparently minor points which are going to become important in the future as collectors become more perceptive. At the present the price is little different from that fetched by any other repoussé watch.

This is another variant of the 'portrait' watch case. The central miniature is again a separate production fitted to a frame but the surrounding decoration is over 'flinqué' enamel. The outer border of white dots may be intended to represent pearls. The price will be a little different from that fetched by the examples on page 88. The ground for 'flinqué' enamel is hand cut whereas the 'guilloche' pattern is produced mechanically.

Musical automata mean money. Ten years ago such a watch might be bought for £500–900, $1,400–2,500, depending on condition and complexity. Today, £1,500–2,500, $4,400–7,500 subject to the same conditions. The small, dancing figures in the centre are decorated with enamel. The pavilion and automata figures in the foreground are of coloured gold. The landscape is painted enamel. The balustrade is not made up of paillons but is champlevé enamel. The best of these watches were made by Piguet and Maylon in Geneva during the first quarter of the 19th Century. A few of them may be earlier but it is doubtful. Mechanical condition will make a big difference to the price owing to the cost of repairs.

This ring watch is included to show the kind of research that can make so much difference to price. By repute and tradition this is the famous repeating watch made by John Arnold and presented to George III. However, there is a certain amount of controversy over the attribution. The under dial work is illustrated in 'The Book of Clocks and Watches', p. 419 figs. 318 a & b, where it is described as 'belonging to George III' and having an 'Eight-day movement': there is no reference to Arnold. The book says that the watch is in the British Museum who also have a ring watch which was at one time supposed to have belonged to George III. There should be no difficulty in proving the association one way or the other as the full details are contained in the 'Annual Register' for 1764. Assuming that this watch was for sale the result of a comparative study between the watch and the Annual Register could mean the difference between a price of £500, $1,500 and £5,000, $15,000. Admittedly this is a particular case but possibly not unique as there are other records of special watches which have yet to be identified.

A mid-18th century repeating watch for the Turkish market. Turkish dials are uncommon at this period and this watch was probably made specially for presentation purposes. The case is set with diamonds and rubies and the quality and quantity of these would determine the price.

The same factors will affect the price of this watch. The inset moss-agate plaques and general decoration point to a slightly earlier date than the last example and are likely to indicate an English watch.
Right
The quality of the ormolu will have more influence on the price than the excellence of the movement.

or watch is sufficiently close in appearance and technique to the work of a famous maker and his signature is added, the picture is quite clear—it is a fake. But what if the signed back plate is used as a basis for a complete clock? Here the signature is quite genuine but the rest is new. Is it a fake or a restoration? Admittedly this is an extreme case and should be considered as faking. But where is the line to be drawn? Obviously some restoration and repair must be expected, but how much? In our extreme case, given that the workman knows his job all the new parts will be made in the correct style and probably by the correct method. While it might be possible for an expert to detect it after a thorough examination, how often can this be done and what is the position of the non-expert dealer who may handle the piece? No real blame can be attached to him as he sells in good faith. At the present time the question of the new, exceptionally over-restored clock or watch rarely occurs. There is more than one reason for this. Even just after the last war there were still sufficient craftsmen to cope with the demand of large scale restoration. Their work was not cheap but costs were well within the possible profit margin. Fragments were comparatively easy to come by at ridiculously low prices and any dealer tended to accumulate large stocks with little or no effort—often in spite of himself. Now the

position has changed. There are fewer skilled craftsmen with the requisite knowledge, they have enough repair work to keep them occupied for many years and few of them are interested in taking on massive restoration work at any price. This is particularly true for clock cases. It is difficult enough to get good repair work done, let alone get a new case made. The supply of raw material is also drying up at an alarming rate, if it has not already done so. Once upon a time, when a dealer died or retired other dealers tried to buy up the whole of the stock, particularly the bits and pieces. Nowadays it is only the front-shop stock which is of interest. The remainder gets sold as scrap or even thrown in the dustbin. Even the contents of the workshop go. This could probably include some valuable old tools. Inevitably there would have been old parts and movements in various stages of disrepair or restoration. Sad as this may be for the historian it is good news for the new collector as it means that the source of new over-restored objects is getting less. This again applies particularly to clocks.

This type of case with its domed top was very popular in the Middle East. The majority have music generally on bells but larger ones may have organs. This one is unusual in that all but one of the four tunes are titled in Turkish ' VALACO ', ' IUSHAL-DENIR ' and ' SABAC-HAFIF '. It is doubtful if this would influence the price! Size and quality will be the deciding factors. It is rare to find a good one for under £750, $2,100 and usually this can be doubled.

A late 18th Century French clock in the form of a miniature secretaire. The front and sides are decorated with painted Sèvres porcelain.   (*Wallace Collection*)

In the watch field the position is much the same although the completely faked watch was never common. Usually it was a matter of fitting an old movement into a new case—rarely the other way round. The made-up watch still occurs with a collection of bits and pieces jumbled together in an effort to produce a credible whole. This rarely succeeds. A small problem arises here: some watches were re-cased and re-dialled by their owners, either because the old case had worn out or become damaged or even just unfashionable. These are quite acceptable and cannot be called fakes. Much of the watch faking has been on the basis of providing false associations by the addition of inscriptions or initials. Today's collector is not naïve. He wants more than just a name engraved on a case. There must be some documentary evidence as well.

Before leaving the subject of fakes, there is one important point to be noted. A fake only becomes a fake when it is discovered to be so. Until then it is perfectly genuine and a good investment! The perfect fake does exist, only to be recognised by its creator and if he should tell someone that he made it he will still not be believed. The forgery can be as difficult to detect as the fake, but this is rarely so. The position is confused by the fact that different makers could and did use the same basic movement. Also one specialist

On the principle that multi-dialled watches may be worth money whatever the period, what is there to look for? At first glance the dial is not all that unusual, the centre-seconds hand and the small button on the band at XII show it to be a fly-back chronograph. The subsidiary dials are mainly for the calendar but the marking on the upper dial show that it is divided for four years. Therefore the calendar work is 'perpetual' and is self correcting for the long and short months. A nice attention to detail is shown in the combined seconds and lunar dial. The zero for the seconds dial corresponds with that for the age of the Moon. The slide on the band is for the repeating work and with a watch of this obvious quality it is safe to assume that it is a minute repeater. Price will vary with maker and condition but a fine example should be nearing the £750, $2,100 mark. An ordinary factory-produced chronograph with simple calendar and quarter repeating would not fetch a tenth of this price.

Centre left

An attractively designed calendar watch of the late 17th Century. The date and age and phase of the Moon are indicated on the two upper dials. The day of the week appears in an aperture within the chapter ring.

(With a decorated case: £250–450, $700–1,400)

Centre right

An exercise in observation. The pendant and ring are obviously wrong and could be improved upon but what after that? From the style of the case, a brass stackfreed movement, possible with steel wheels. Certainly a clock watch, from the pierced case and the hole in the dial, on the right by V. Possibly quarter-striking and/or alarum. The quarter-strike is suspected from the central quarter-cum-minute hand which is not usual at this period. Neither is the 24 hour dial divided I–XII twice. The ring just inside the chapters is probably for the alarum. The central part of the dial is a lunar calendar showing the age and phase with the astrological aspect. At present it shows that the moon is 16 days old, waning and in opposition; naturally it is in quadrature and sexpartiture as well but these do not count. Date, from general impressions, end of 16th and beginning of 17th Century. The movement may have neither signature nor punchmark. Price today, assuming a good movement, over £2,000 $5,600. The reason for taking all this trouble in forecasting what might be inside is 'gamesmanship'. So far the seller cannot know how interested you may be in this watch. He may not know how important this watch is but you have already guessed and you know roughly what to expect when it is opened. This you can confirm with the minimum of apparent interest and this can keep the price down.

A late popular revival of the so-called pendulum watch. The arm carrying the bob is geared off the escapement. The case is likely to be silver rather than gold. Most of these were made for export to China in the 19th Century.

(£5–40, $14–110)

This is again more Regency ornament than clock. It is really an elaborated watch and probably needs winding each day. The quarter-seconds and centre-seconds are reminiscent of the Chinese market watches but this is for the home market. This type of clock has only gone up in price during the last six or seven years. £60–500, $168–1,400 for one in good condition and of top quality. Always examine these clocks carefully as many have suffered the ravages of time and have been badly restored. Some may even have later movements.

might work for more than one maker so that two identical watches may be found with different names on them. Both are genuine in that they were commissioned and sold by the man whose name appears on the dial and movement. A plain case of honest sub-contracting—not forgery. In some instances it was this sub-contracting which led to forgery. A maker might break into a foreign market. As his trade expanded he had to subcontract to keep abreast of the increasing demand. The sub-contractor often branched out on his own and tried to cut out what he considered as the middle man, by producing his own version and exporting it direct. So it is possible to find one maker's name on three versions of the same watch. The original model, the sub-contracted version and the forgery. A practised eye is needed to differentiate the first two but the third is usually easily recognised. For some reason, probably price, the sub-contracted model was not an exact copy. The forgery extended to the hall-marks in the case, often with ludicrous results. This was forgery on a large scale and aimed at different markets at different periods. At about the end of the 18th Century it was Russia and Turkey. Later it was the turn of the U.S.A. but there the general style of the native watch was copied rather than a particular maker. It even worked in reverse with Waterbury watches being copied in Europe. In recent times the Swiss have been the victims. The firm of Rolex in particular. The work of famous makers was forged on a somewhat smaller scale. Sometimes it was not so much a case of copying a man's work but merely signing his name. In general this is true of most forgeries. The name is the same and that is all. The reproduction field is vast, particularly where furnishing clocks are concerned but there is little danger of these being mistaken for antiques as long as

This type of watch might be called a visual repeater. There is no dial in the usual sense of the word, and the time is indicated by the two pointers held by the figure but these move only when the pendant is pressed. There is another type in which the arms move continuously. These watches do not turn up often enough to quote comparative prices, but today £750, $2,100 would not be unreasonable.

A dial like this presents an immediate problem. The answer could make the difference between £40, $112 and £1,500, $4,200! It could even be found on a silver-cased watch when the lowest price would be, at least halved. The double dials for the hours can be found on cheap verge watches and were intended, as they are today, to show the time in two places and so save the traveller the inconvenience of altering his watch. Such watches may have the seconds hand mounted centrally or be on a subsidiary dial rarely both and often neither. The duplicated seconds-hands often mean a watch with independent seconds and are separately connected to its own hour dial. The price will depend on the maker and the technical details of the movement.

they have their original movements. But many of the cases are often good enough to pass for antique when a period movement is fitted. However, the cases will not stand up to a close examination, nor will the mounts and hinges. Lantern clocks were also made extensively but the metal used was of a much lighter gauge than the original and it was rolled rather than hammered. The thickness and texture is too uniform. The wheels and pinions do not stand up to comparison with genuine work. This does not

A mid-18th Century French wall clock.
(Wallace Collection)

apply of course to those lantern clocks with spring-driven movements of the kind that are still being sold. Probably the most famous reproductions were of the water clocks that were produced in Birmingham. One version is still being made. These have been completely accepted and can be seen for sale at prices up to and including £500, $1,400. As a matter of interest some models are rarer than others and might be worth buying at the right price.

The most famous of the reproduction watches were produced in Vienna at the end of the 19th Century. At one time these watches were too completely believed and fetched relatively high prices. The price dropped when they were recognised for what they were but today it is climbing again as they gradually become antiques in their own right. Perhaps reproduction is not the right word for these watches as they do not seem to have been intended as copies of any known form of antique watch except perhaps some of those in so called crystal cases and even those are more 'in the style of' than direct imitations. The Viennese watches, and incidentally small clocks, all feature enamel in one form or another. The glass watches were usually octagonal or oval but some egg-shaped ones are found. The mounts are of silver gilt decorated with a fairly simple design in brightly coloured opaque and transparent enamels. The dials are in champlevé enamel resembling the bird and flower pattern of the earlier 17th Century but in more garish colours. If the clocks can be said to follow any precedent, they follow, though vaguely, the more exotic productions of the 17th Century on the one hand, and the confections of James Cox on the other. But these are on a smaller scale. Monstrance clocks, classical figures supporting watches, small cabinets topped off with a small watch and other fancies. The decoration, painted champlevé enamel, on a silver gilt ground, is the same as on other Viennese products of the time. The painting is quite good but unmistakably of the 19th Century. There was, however, a large production of true reproduction watches. These fall roughly into two groups. Those which were mass produced and the ones that were almost individual productions. Somewhere in between there were a few that were hand finished from a standardised set of parts. Perhaps some of the individual productions deserve the title of fake, in that they are often signed with the name of a famous maker but with no regard to that particular maker's style or the ornament of his period. It is hard to believe today that anybody ever thought of them as anything but reproductions. That they did take them to be genuine can be seen by looking through the illustrations in the earlier books and sale catalogues.

Not only metal was used but materials not normally associated with watch work. Ivory was a particular favourite. Also wood, although wooden watches were actually produced in 19th Century Russia by Bronikoff and can now fetch three figures depending on their condition and completeness. Some of the mass-produced reproductions are so crude as to be practically valueless even as curiosities. The metal work is badly finished with rough edges, the gilding is poor and the lines of the decoration are usually dotted rather than engraved. Very few of these have survived. A more credible series of reproductions were produced in Munich at the end of the 19th Century. Their best feature was the case. The dials are naïve and the movements unbelievable. They consist only of a silver back-plate, engraved to resemble the back-plate of a watch. This plate is supported by slender pillars fixed to the back of the dial. An 18th or 19th Century movement is fitted between the dial and back-plate. Sometimes the back-plate is cut away in the centre to reveal the back of the fitted movement which may then be engraved with the name of an early 17th Century maker. The cases are good enough to deceive the beginner. They may be oval or tambour shaped. The bands may be pierced or enamelled, the lids can be silver, pierced and engraved, or engraved glass, but they all have one thing in common. They are decorated with a circular medallion of the crucifixion. Over £1,000, $2,800 has been asked for the high grade model, an oval watch with an enamel band and dial, engraved glass lids and signed movement. But the current price seems to have settled at between £10–50, $30–150 depending on the type.

Reproduction stackfreed watches in tambour cases were made in Amsterdam until the beginning of the last war. The movements are flimsy with thin wheels and plates and two small pinions. Sometimes examination will show

Strangely the addition of a matching châtelaine does not always mean a great increase in the price of a gold repoussé cased watch although they will fetch more together than as individual items. This does not apply when it is obvious that the two have always belonged together. This example dates from about 1750 and the open form of the plaques forming the châtelaine is rarer than the price would suggest.

(£170–350, $500–1,250)

This is an unusual combination. The watch is decorated with coloured gold set against an enamel background imitating bloodstone. The châtelaine also has coloured gold decoration but it is applied to blued steel. The rarity is reflected in the price which is more than it would have been if it were all gold.

(£200–450, $580–1,260)

A gold mounted moss-agate watch and châtelaine of about 1750 with the original crank-key. They may not belong together as the scroll-work of the châtelaine lacks the architectural details found in the watch case. This would make little difference to the price.

(£400–850, $1,150–2,400)

Another unusual type of decoration especially on the case which is of grey agate with applied gold scenic decoration set with diamonds, emeralds and rubies.

(£1,000–2,500, $3,000–7,500)

This could be a real investment and should not take very long to produce a good profit. The enamel is on copper and is English, probably Staffordshire. These cases and châtelaines have largely missed the attention of the enamel collectors. A rather similar case can be found in porcelain but at about ten times the price.

(£100–240, $220–700)

A really exotic 18th Century watch and châtelaine of the kind usually found on watches by Cabrier. Gold, mother-of-pearl, diamonds, rubies and enamel; complete with the original key and seal. This would be an expensive but safe investment, as the price is very unlikely to drop. Against that the increases are erratic, they may stand still for some time and then take a sudden jump. It is doubtful whether it could have been bought for under £1,000, $3,000 ten years ago. Today it will fetch something over £2,500, $7,000.

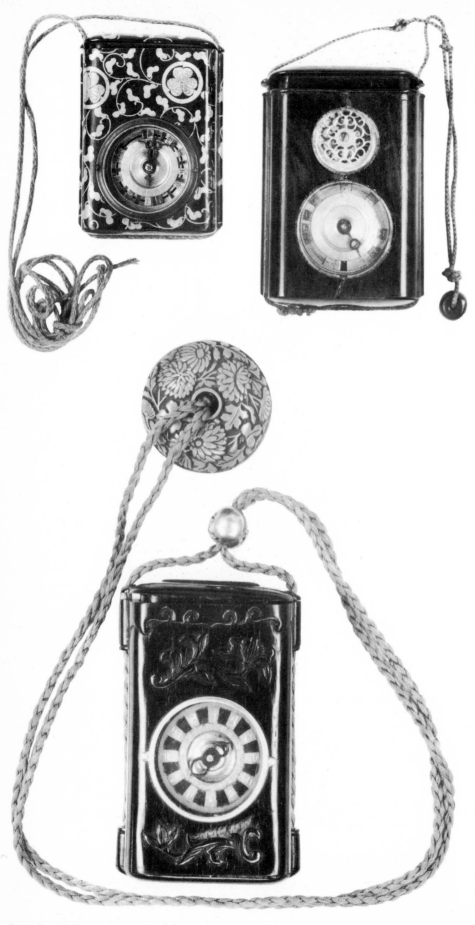

The Japanese 'inro' watch rarely appears in the salerooms and may well be overlooked in shops dealing in oriental antiques. In general the average price ten years ago was under £100, $280 but much depended on the decoration and whether or not it was a clock-watch. In most instances the movement is a miniaturised clock. The cord should pass through a small bead, the ojime, and have a larger ornament, the 'netsuke', at its end. The absence of these ornaments does not greatly affect the price as they may be replaced with little difficulty if not expense. Sometimes the dial may revolve behind a fixed hand but the hour numerals are always adjustable to suit the Japanese system which had hours of varying length. The fact that this is a clock-watch and has a well decorated case will more than make up for the lack of ojime and netsuke. Today's price at a minimum would be £350, $1,250.

The visible balance indicates that this Japanese inro is not a clock-watch but the fact that it is visible will help compensate for this and the plainness of the case.
(£175, $500)

This Japanese watch is complete in every detail. However its relative plainness will keep the price down to about £250, $700.

that the trains could never have run. The cases are often pierced although no bell is fitted or even needed. Pierced cases which are not on clock or alarum watches should always be subjected to the closest scrutiny when they are encountered. It is possible that they may be genuine old cases housing later movements and not always fakes.

There remains one last series of watches which have been completely accepted and which formed the subject matter of a book, which is today extremely rare. The book was written by the man who actually produced these watches for the trade for a period of years and who considered that he deserved a larger share of the profits. When this was not forthcoming he wrote the book as a form of blackmail. That this was successful is shown by the scarcity of the book. Most of the copies were quickly bought up and destroyed as the author had intended. This book is the basis of research at the present time and a new edition has been proposed. The products of this man could be called the watches that never were, as they are modifications of French and Swiss watches of the later 18th and early 19th Centuries. One of the most popular of the models was a form of the pornographic automaton

A late 18th Century mantel clock in Sèvres porcelain. *(Wallace Collection)*

repeater. In the original the automaton forms part of a Jacquemart repeater concealed beneath a double shutter which appears below the enamel chapter-ring. The shutter is opened by a slide in the band of the case. Sometimes the shutter carried, appropriately enough, a model of a goat which nodded its head when the repeating train was running and incidently gave the required motion to the concealed automaton. Human nature being what it is these watches were popular and the demand has always been greater than the supply. It is obviously difficult to remodel a Jacquemart repeater so that the automaton can be fitted in the usual place and an easier solution was found. A hole was cut in the centre of the curvette or inner dome. This received a shallow box containing the automaton. The lid of the box was released by a small push in the rim of the curvette. The requisite movement was supplied by a small crank mounted on the extended pivot of a wheel in the repeating train. Clearly this device could be fitted to any type of repeater. The only drawback was that the back of the watch had to be opened first before the automaton could be seen. Other less lurid modifications were produced, usually connected with the dial and the way of indicating the time. It is not anticipated that any new edition of the exposé will have any effect on the price of these watches.

The French made ornate musical clocks although the carillon was often what might be considered as a separate construction and indeed would exist on its own. Even those found together were not always mechanically connected and the music had to be let off when it was wanted rather than playing at fixed intervals of time. Sometimes the musical movement is missing and sometimes the two halves have been married at a later date. As with all French clocks the price will depend on its decorative value.

Today this is nothing more than an ornament and will be priced accordingly. It
will be bought by a porcelain collector who
will not be unduly worried if it does not
have a movement let alone keep time.

Collectors and dealers will occasionally declare something to be a fake even
when it is genuine. The reason is not always to lower the price so that they
can buy cheaply. They may not want it themselves but will damn a clock
or watch to spoil the reputation of whoever does buy it or to cast doubt on the
integrity of the seller. For this reason and in the final analysis the best
protection for the buyer is his own knowledge which he can only get by
practical experience. Horology has not yet received the mass attention of a
great body of experts. There has been no one to sit in judgement on clocks
and watches in the same way as on paintings, porcelain, sculpture, enamels,
silver and the like. The sheep and goats are still milling around
together and the investor must to a great extent be his own detective.

AREAS FOR INVESTMENT

The difficult advice to provide is where the investor of modest means should put his money. General suggestions are not enough but if a particular line is indicated the adviser risks his reputation. Also it could result in a false rise in the price of certain clocks and watches which might or might not continue. Hindsight is easy—anyone can tell you what you should have bought in 1950. There was even quite a good chance of saying it in 1950 itself when there were more specialist dealers and more of the junk shops and stalls that were the happy hunting-ground for both dealer and collector. Nowadays there are fewer clocks and watches, especially those selling for shillings rather than pounds. The lower the price, the smaller the selection becomes. But if we make the usual division between the decorative and the technical it may be possible to make a few guesses at what the horological collector may be looking for in 1980. The upper price limit will be set at about £50, $140 but many purchases will be possible for as many shillings.

Opposite

These 19th century enamels can still be bought for well under £100, $280. Not so long ago eyebrows were raised if they fetched as much as £20, $56.

The decoration is a mixture of champlevé and basse-taille techniques and is finally covered with a transparent flux.

(£60, $170)

The flowers in the centre are painted champlevé enamel and are a miniature version of those on the back of the earlier Chinese export watches. Because the area of the enamel decorated is quite small the price is still quite low.

(£35, $100)

This can almost be classified as a form watch. The enamelling technique is the same as that used on the last. The shape adds something to the price.

(£75, $210)

Basically the technique is similar except that the figures are in graduated blue.

(£45, $130)

The gold scrollwork round the painted picture is not foil but the gold of the case. The covering glaze stops before the scroll-work round the edge of the case.

(£60, $170)

This page

Left

Silver or gold piqué cases will always add to a watch's value. The case alone can fetch upwards of £20, $50 in silver or £30, $100 in gold according to the age and quality. To judge from the decoration this case is French of about 1690. The holes round the edge show that it was intended for an alarum or clock watch.

Right

This type of case is usually on a Chinese export watch. The tortoiseshell has been slightly underpainted. The existence of such a case on the matching watch would add about £5, $14.

Firstly the decorative. It is still possible to buy small, enamelled gold watches for upwards of £25, $70—this applies to later 18th Century examples with additional coloured gold decorations as well as the 19th Century ladies' pendant watches. These watches should be very carefully scrutinised as condition is all important. Look for scratched enamel and rubbed engraving, bad catches and worn hinges. The mid-Victorian engraved, gold cased watches, both hunters and open faced, will also appreciate, particularly those with pictorial decorations. Many of these are copies of contemporary engravings and can be traced to the originals. It does not seem likely that watches with straightforward floral engravings will rise in price for many years unless they are of the type which have the ground filled with enamel, usually black. Silver cased watches of the same period are quite cheap but there does not seem to be any future for them as investments except when considered over a very long period. A point to be checked when buying these watches is whether there is a name on them anywhere, as the anonymous watch is always at a disadvantage. The name usually engraved on the inner dome is rarely that of the manufacturer but as the historian begins to document this period, these names may turn out to be significant. For the more technically minded, it is often possible to identify the actual makers from the

Opposite

The pendant is probably Viennese and late 19th Century but the case is of another type usually credited to the elder Pierre Huaud. The floral painting is visibly better than the portrait, while the feathered head-dress is considered to be particularly typical of Huaud. These watches are much rarer than those signed by the sons, and there are no reliable recorded prices. This Pierre Huaud died in 1680.

The type of dial which could be found on the last example.

The inclusion of small brilliants in the decoration of this 'portrait' watch indicates a later date than those illustrated elsewhere but the price would be virtually the same.

Examples of later 18th Century enamelled cases. The backs were often manufactured separately and set into gold or gilt-metal frames. The metal of the base for the enamel is normally copper but may be gold. With a little practice it becomes possible to make a good guess at the metal used: for the watch at the left of the centre row it is probably gold, for those in the bottom row, copper. The central one of these is an unusual type. All would be approximately in the same price bracket, with an appropriate allowance for gold.

(£30–80, $85–230)

The signature 'Les deux frères Huaut pintre de son A-E a berlin' enables this case to be dated between 1686, when Jean-Pierre and Amy Huaud went to Berlin as painters to the Court of Prussia and 1700 when they returned to Geneva. These two Huauds were the younger brothers of Pierre, son of the elder Pierre. Huaud watches are not all that uncommon but really good examples are getting rare and the price is rising steadily. The gold piqué outer case might add to the price.

(£500–1,000, $1,500–3,000)

This page

A late 17th Century outer case, coloured with tortoiseshell and decorated with silver. This was made for an alarum watch or perhaps a clock-watch. It should not be on an ordinary watch. Such a case should lift the price of the right watch by £10–20, $26–56.

Right

Such an outer case belongs on a watch made around 1675 or possibly a little earlier. The leather should be in good condition, the nails may be gold or silver. For silver add £15–25, $42–70 to the price of the watch, for gold £25–40, $70–112. Naturally the metal of the outer and inner cases should match. Condition is very important and repairs are almost impossible unless you do them yourself.

design of the movement. As some of these firms are direct ancestors of today's famous firms, it would be an advantage to be able to say that the movement of a certain watch was made by Charles Smith Ltd. who after became the Alphex Watch Co., makers of the timing equipment used in the 1975 moon rocket, so that some attention to the design of the movement is indicated. This may sound far fetched but a moment's thought and a quick look at current watch advertising will show that the first moves have already been made in this direction. The most obvious investment is the so called Art Nouveau clock or watch. Very few true Art Nouveau objects are to be found. Most of them date from around 1925 although some watches are of 1905 vintage. Little or no interest has been shown in the horology of this period and it would seem to offer a good opportunity to judge by what is happening in other fields in the Art Nouveau world. Chapuis's book *The Swiss Watch* has illustrations of engraved, cast, enamel and gem set watches of this period

which give a good idea of what to look for. At the present time these are more likely to be found in jewellery sales with many forming part of job lots.

The late 18th, early 19th Century base metal enamelled watches seem to show possibility. Some people consider these to be garish, especially when they are set with pastes, but good examples should appreciate. 18th Century silver cased watches with painted enamel dials have doubled in price in five years. In some instances the price has reached as high as £25, $70, even higher in the U.S.A. It seems to be governed by a subject. Pastoral scenes are the least valued. Railway trains top the list. This 'scenic value' also applies to some enamel cases. Ballooning scenes fetch a premium, especially if it is possible to identify a particular balloon or episode. Motoring scenes can also be found on cases. Some of these were for presentation use but others were ordinary production models somewhat like the 'railway timekeepers' with magnificent engines on the backs of their cases. Somewhere there must be some cases with aeroplanes on them! Contemporary clocks do not seem to have a comparable decorative appeal except of course those coming under the general description of Art Nouveau. The price of these will probably go up like a rocket for a while and then level off. Although they were mass-produced, very few have survived so that they have become

The typical 'Puritan' watch case is normally made of silver and has usually lost its
outer case. This one has an additional
indication for the date surrounding the
chapter ring. These watches were made
about 1630–40 and a premium is usually
paid for watches made by the members of
the Worshipful Company of Clockmakers
which was formed during this period. These
watches can be found in gold, silver cased
watches would bring a little over half the
price quoted.

(£450–1,000, $1,250–3,000)

The standard 'drum clock with alarum
attachment', although the dial is not
exactly conventional. Ten years ago eye-
brows would rise if such a clock fetched
£100, $280. Today that figure could be
multiplied by seven or eight.

rarities today. Probably the later 19th Century furnishing clocks will also
eventually become collectors' items, but not soon enough to be considered as
investments now. The exceptions will be the novelty clocks. The
'engineering' clocks are moving already. Beam engines, boilers, steam
hammers, reciprocating engines, railway engines, motor cars, light-houses,
all having moving parts, are already above the £50, $140 mark and show no
signs of slackening. Nothing else seems to provide a reasonable chance of
being a reliable clock investment. Carriage and skeleton clocks are already
beyond the reach of the small investor.

The technical side of clockmaking offers little of interest for a small outlay
except perhaps the later electrical clocks. Most of the early ones are already
nearing the £100, $280 and some have passed this figure.

Much more was happening in the world of watchmaking in the 19th
Century, some of which has survived for the benefit for the small investor,
if his lack of money is compensated for by knowledge and imagination. It
was the age of invention and saw the rise of mass-production which made the
cheap watch a possibility. In fact, the mass-production was only an extension
of the earlier batch production which was responsible for the antique watches
already sought after today, and as the everyday watch of the 18th Century is
now steadily rising in price, it should follow that the typical 19th Century
watch will go the same way. The big difference seems to be that the 19th
Century offers a bigger variety. The cylinder had largely replaced the verge as
the common escapement and so the collector's attention should turn to the early
levers. The lever escapement was being developed throughout the century
and there were many varieties. In the second half of the century certain
designs came to indicate particular firms and these will gradually become
sought after as they become recognised. The same will apply to the complete
movements supplied by people like Victor Kullberg, Nicole Nielson and
Hector Golay. The introduction and perfection of keyless mechanism, self
winding watches and chronographs also provide opportunities for building
up valuable collections for a small outlay. The same applies to the early and
sometimes unorthodox models of firms like Rolex, Omega, Longines, Le
Coultre, Vacheron and Constantin and others. There are also the firms that
failed and which are part of the history of horology. Examples from these
should be sought out. Occasional examples of the watches made by these
firms can be found on barrows, some in good enough condition to be considered as collectors' items, but the derelict ones should not be neglected.
They are a source of spare parts. If this sounds like collecting junk, it is just

that. But the later silver pair cased verges which could be bought for scrap prices a little over ten years ago now cost at least £3, $9. A two thousand per cent rise is not to be sneered at. Certain novelty watches can still be bought relatively cheaply. For instance later examples of the chronoscope with pin

It is difficult to forecast the future of the long-case clock. There is no reason to think that there will be any drop in the prices of really good specimens and as well designed clocks by lesser known makers are still good furniture they will probably gain in price at a quicker rate and may be the better investment for a smaller outlay. Today a clock like this would be about £900, $2,500.

A big clock over nine feet tall! Even though it goes for a year on one winding its size will keep the price down to about £300–500 $840–1,400. At this price it would be a good buy if you had somewhere to put it.

A good example of a mid-18th Century enamel dial. Earlier dials have heavier markings. Later the external minute numerals were to disappear.

A late example (1780) of the old tradition of repoussé work. It is somewhat crude and the price suffers accordingly.

(£50–70, $140–190)

On this type of oval watch the movement is slipped in from the front and secured by two latches on either side of the dial. Here the chapter ring is engraved on the dial-plate but there can be a separate ring or complete dial riveted to the plate. Early 17th Century.

(£150–300, $400–850.
Case alone: about £100, $275)

Ring watches are always good investments especially if the movement is in good enough condition to keep reasonable time. This is an early 17th Century example with a visible balance.

(£200–500, $500–1,750)

The small disc in the centre of the dial is used for setting the alarum. The square hinge is a feature of the late 17th Century. This watch is Dutch but it could just as easily be English. These champlevé dials are also found on German and Genevan watches. The maker's name is important, a watch by Tompion will cost about three times more than one by a lesser maker even if the movements are virtually identical. The price of such a watch in a silver case has varied but a little over the last ten years but is beginning to rise.

(£35–55, $100–200)

A repeating watch in gold pair-cases. About 1730–40. A rare type with an allegorical decoration. It is interesting to see that Father Time is holding the symbol of eternity in his left hand. This type of case was not appreciated ten years ago. It would be most unusual to find a signature on a case like this but it falls within the period that includes the work of many makers whose names fetch a premium.

(£35–200, $90–550)

The second half of the 18th Century saw quite a few of these gold mounted, hardstone cases still being made. Most of them were for ordinary watches. This one is for a repeater and is decorated with an applied floral spray set with diamonds and rubies. The condition of the movement is less important than that of the case.

(£250–1,000, $1,000–3,000)

Today an outer case of silver filigree can add £50–75, $150–250 to the price. A similar case in gold would cost about twice as much.

Subsidiary seconds dials started to appear soon after the introduction of the balance-spring about 1675. Early examples are collector's items, especially those by a maker like Tompion.

(£120–700, $330–2,000)

These early 19th Century coloured gold cases whose decoration is preserved under a glazed cover have been neglected and the price has barely doubled in the last decade. Today they may still be bought for about £60, $170 which is ridiculously low.

The 'Barking Dog' is a sought after variant of the repeating watch. These watches are rarer in silver cases than in gold but far less valuable. The dog 'Barks' the hours and quarters. The best ones are wind operated with a small circular bellows visible from the back. The cheaper version has a kind of mechanical rasp to produce the noise. Today a good example should go over £1,000, $2,800.

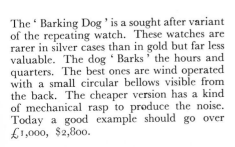

pallet movements, aperture watches by the International Watch Company,
cheap musical alarm watches or railway guards' watches with the name or
initials of the company on the back or dial. Any of these may be found at
prices under £10, $28. So can 18th Century verge watches with decorated
outer cases covered in tortoise shell, particularly the ones with under-painting.
Even with an upper price limit of £50, $140, the investor is beset with the
problem of what not to buy, as many watches which are nearly right come
within this price range. When in doubt only pay a price that could be expected for a genuine movement or case. Cases alone are worth buying, not
necessarily with a view to marrying them to a watch but as decorative objects
in their own right. Anyone who feels he must collect names might well try
some of the lesser known makers: Van Ceulen, Pieter Visbach, Isaac Thuret,
Jacob Frisard, Tixier, Albert Potter, the Howard Watch Company, Paul
Ditisheim, Thomas Russell and the various Glashütte firms. A little imagination and research will soon provide more names. Admittedly this can be
a gamble, but any buying with a real purpose in mind rarely is.

Apart from the actual clocks and watches and of course the literature on
the subject, there are all the allied objects: watch cocks, fobs, keys, watch

A mid-17th Century verge movement
showing the backplate and cock, above,
and below, the fusee.

132

papers, alarm and repeating attachments, stands, tools. Many of these fields have not been exploited. Collection of watch cocks, the decorative brackets holding the upper pivot of the balance, have been formed and dispersed but little has been done recently. It is well known that large numbers of cocks were made into jewellery in Victorian times. The demand became so great that cast reproductions were made. These are practically valueless and should not be bought. They are easy to detect. The edges of the piercing are rough, there is no pivot hole and the electro-gilding rarely compares with the old mercurial gilding. As a matter of interest, some of these reproductions may be found on actual watches where they have been used to replace a cock which had been removed to make jewellery. The early examples of watch cocks are sought after most, and a good example of the 17th Century pinned on cock can fetch upwards of £10, $28. The late 18th and early 19th Century cocks are not particularly interesting. But even these have increased their price by about six hundred per cent in the last ten years. Cut steel fobs and chains are getting very scarce now but can still be found in some of the old established country jewellers. It is always worth asking. The more decorative short châtelaines have already passed out of range for the average man but there are possibilities in the ornamental gold chains of the second half of the 19th Century. Watches need keys to wind them; where possible contemporary keys are best even if they are not intended to form a collection. Keys come in all sorts of shapes and sizes, some are more valuable than others but the condition should be good unless the type is rare. A few years ago these

Right
Traditionally the name of James Cox is usually associated with clocks of this type. They may not bear his name but they are certainly in the same idiom as those clocks exhibited in the Museum in Spring Gardens. This museum was dispersed by public Lottery. These clocks vary in size and luxury and this will influence the price which has been rising steadily. Today a relatively uninspired example would fetch about £850, $2,650.

Left
This clock is included to confuse the issue. It was probably made in China, in imitation of the European clocks, in about 1780–1830. The movement may even be engraved with a curious meander intended to be the maker's signature. The clocks can vary between £250, $700 for a very plain one to £3,000, $8,400 for one of the grand musical automata.

were sought after to put on charm bracelets. Now that that fashion has passed there is a chance of finding quite good keys in trays of small antique and curio shops. The so called gem set ones must be in nearly mint condition to be worth buying, but look for the uncommon, such as silver crank keys, especially the jointed type, and form keys, particularly revolvers and rifles. One type that has been almost completely neglected was made up as advertising for jewellers and bore their names and addresses.

There are advertisements of another form which are well worth investing in, if recent prices are any indication. These are the watch papers. Their price has risen something like 800% in less than five years, but naturally this does not apply to all of them. The best are those of the better known watch makers, and ones which include equation tables and decorative features typical of certain periods. Foreign examples are rare. Not all watch papers are advertising material, neither are they always made of paper: some are printed on satin, others are embroidered—lace and crochet were also used and also cut paper. These last can be so extremely delicate that is it a wonder that they have survived. The watch paper is to be found in the outer case of the pair cased watch. Unfortunately, many have been thrown away as rubbish. Today the price ranges between a 1/- and about £5 (15c–$15). So a pair cased watch may yield an unexpected dividend. One of the problems of displaying a watch collection can be overcome by the use of antique watch stands which may be functional as well as highly decorative. Many of the more elaborate ones were specially made for rich collectors as display stands. This seems to make no difference to their appeal or to their price. The majority are plain wooden arches supported by turned columns fitted into a round base. This type progresses to those covered with tortoiseshell and with ivory capitals and bases. Some were made in gilt-metal but these are seldom attractive. The best of the metal stands are very ornate and stand on a rather flat tripod base. The watch is visible through a circular aperture in the middle of rococo scroll work and held in place by a spring clip. Some of these were made by Matthew Boltland and even these can be still found at about £30, $85. The French Empire ormulu stands are already over our limit, especially the eagles with outspread wings with the hook for the watch held in their beaks. However, there are still some attractive wooden stands to be found, and may be either carved ones which are mostly Continental or others modelled on contemporary clock cases. One of these types is well worth looking for. It is roughly like a true bracket clock but made almost in one piece. The bracket has a strut at the back to hang it on the wall and the case slides down over the strut. The case and bracket have ebonised mouldings and are veneered in tortoiseshell. The interesting feature is the plaque at the front which surrounds the watch. This is cast in a break arch form so that it gives the impression of a clock dial when the watch is in place. The arch contains a portrait medallion of one of the 18th Century monarchs.

There are also the tools which are used to make and repair these clocks and watches. Unfortunately, many of these have been bought up by the interior decorators and are sold at fairly high prices. But this is a fashion that will pass and the investor will have his chance. Naturally, the decorator has concentrated on the larger and more impressive tools which are less likely to get lost and so will come on the market later. The smaller tools can still be found in some of the older jeweller's shops providing you can persuade the owners to look for them. Britten's *Handbook*, already referred to, will help you to identify any tools you may find.

Finally, a few general points that apply particularly to the investor with financial limitations. Never guess; if you do not know, ask somebody's advice, check and then make up your own mind. Never buy at random, always have a buying policy—unless you can afford to be a magpie. Always buy the best you can afford, and if you cannot afford it leave it alone. You may have to liquidate in a hurry and probably at a loss. If you do make a loss, try to find out where you went wrong. If after buying something you find that you have made a mistake, get rid of it. If you find a good source of supply, look after it. But if you see something which you know is of interest to someone else, tell them. With any luck they will do the same for you. Goodwill always pays dividends, and today's unconsidered trifle will be tomorrow's antique.

There are two forms of crystal crucifix watches; some are made entirely of crystal, but this one (*c.* 1640) has a metal frame to hold the stone. The crystal watches were more rarely reproduced than those in metal cases. Most of these are betrayed by their piercing.

(£500–900, $1,400–2,500)

The Memento Mori watch came into use at the beginning of the 17th Century and was made over a period of about sixty years. Most of the cases are silver but some were made from rock crystal. The lower jaw and bottom of the skull are usually in one piece and are hinged to reveal the dial of the watch. The price does not vary a great deal but exceptionally large or small examples may fetch more. Skull watches should be examined carefully as reproductions were made in the 19th Century.

(£350–750, $1,000–2,500)

The long pointed oval cases are mostly Dutch or English from the late 16th and early 17th Centuries. Of the two the English version would probably fetch a slightly higher price but would not go as high as a watch fitted with a stackfreed.

(£250–1,000, $700–3,000)

A calendar watch in cast silver case, almost certainly English about 1660–70 although by that time it would be a little old fashioned. The date is shown by a pointer on the rotating steel ring surrounding the chapters. It is unusual to find a case with a complete lid as late as this. The price could be lower in America where Continental watches of this period seem to fetch more.

(£175–350, $450–1,000)

An early 17th Century oval watch. It could be English in spite of the numerals 13–24 engraved within the main chapters I–XII. The case is of gilt-metal. The condition of the movement is important but even a relic may be worth about £150, $375.

(£300–750, $850–2,100)

BIBLIOGRAPHY

Although books can be thought as the basic tools of the research worker, and consequently the investor, they can be more than just that. Horological books wisely bought can be investments in themselves. This can be seen by comparing the original cost of some of the standard books which are now out of print with today's prices. This rise in price is even more noticeable with those books that have been out of print for many years. In some instances they are luxuries to the general collector, but others are almost indispensable and as it is most unlikely that any of these will ever be superceded their value can be expected to rise. Most of the earlier books are in French or German, both of which languages are almost essential to the study of horology. Although there are a great many books in English they do not cover the subject completely. The completely indispensable book is *Watch-makers and Clock-makers of the World* by G. H. Baillie containing some 35,000 names of craftsmen working in all parts of the world before about 1825. In general it is quite reliable and gives information on the whereabouts of some comparative material. There is no international list of makers working after 1825 and this information is difficult to find. It is unlikely that such a list will ever be compiled and published but some specialised books have been printed and others are in preparation and may ease the problem in certain fields.

For American makers Brook Palmer's *Book of American Clocks* (1950) is generally reliable as a basic guide. But collectors of Americana are recommended to join the National Association of Watch and Clock Collectors (P.O. Box 33, Columbia, Pa.) who run a good information service for their members. Palmer's book was remaindered some years ago and it can still be bought quite cheaply. It is worth buying as there are no signs that it will be replaced in the foreseeable future. Specialised local books have been written on the makers of Connecticut and Pennsylvania.

There is no separate and complete list of French makers. One was prepared but it has not, as yet, been published. Nor is it likely that it will be. There are two excellent books on the makers of Blois and Lyons and the odd pamphlet on other centres. *Vial and Cote, Les Horlogers Lyonnais de* 1550 à 1650 (1927) and *Develle, Les Horlogers Blesois au* 16 *et au* 17 *siècle* (1913) are both models of definitive works on makers and districts. The only area of revision lies in the list of clocks and watches still extant and their locations, as many of the pieces quoted were in private collections since dispersed. Also other examples have come to light since the books were written. In addition to the actual watch-makers they have details of the ancillary trades of case-maker and enameller. For general information on the earlier French makers the indispensable book is *L'Horlogerie Ancienne* by Edouard Gélis (1949). The Gélis book is out of print and the price is steadily rising. At present it is around the £10 mark ($30 to $35) and worth buying. It contains a good bibliography. For many years Edouard Gélis worked on the Garnier and Olivier collections, now in the Louvre and the Musée des Arts Decoratif. His own collection is on view in the Musée Saint-Reymond in Toulouse.

The Swiss, particularly Alfred Chapuis have produced their fair share of books but no separate list of makers. The standard work by Chapuis and Jaquet is *The Swiss Watch* (1956). This also was remaindered although not for the usual reasons, and can still be found occasionally at £5 to £6 ($25 to $35 in the U.S.A.).

There is no authoritative general book on Germanic clockmaking in spite of the huge horological literature, most of which appears in periodicals. The trouble here is that the field is vast and needs to be broken down. Separate books on Augsburg, Nuremberg, Dresden and Vienna would be a help if they included only those clocks and watches which could be definitely attributed to those towns. Most of the basic research has already been done. It is just a matter of bringing it together.

Italian clocks and watches particularly the early examples are good investments. Here the difficulty lies in separating them from the work of the southern German makers and some of the French clock makers of the south-eastern area. A preliminary list of makers, *Dizionario degli Orologiai* (1950) has been compiled by Enrico Morpurgo which also contains a large bibliography of source material.

Nanne Ottema's *Geschiedenis van de Uurwekmakerskunst in Friesland* (1948) is the basic and only extant list of Dutch makers. But a new book is being

A clock commissioned by the city of Avignon and presented to the Marquis de Rochechouart in 1771. The design is an elaborate allegory of Avignon and its geographical situation. *(Wallace Collection)*

A French gilt bronze cylindrical clock.
The time is indicated by the small arrow.
About 1780.   *(Wallace Collection)*

A French clock of about 1780 representing Love Triumphing over the Flight of Time. Shown here from the back. The movement is contained in the globe which is enamelled dark blue. *(Wallace Collection)*

prepared by John Leopold of the Groningen Museum. This book contains examples of the work of the various makers in addition to biographical details.

Scandinavian horology is an unexplored field, largely because few of their clocks and fewer of their watches appear on the market. As far as the Swedish makers are concerned, the only book is *Urmakare i Sverige under Äldre Tider* (1947) by Elis Sidenbladh.

These are the basic books supplying information on the makers and their dates. They help first to determine the authenticity of the particular item actually bought or under consideration. At the same time they may give some idea of its importance and comparative rarity and provide some guide to its possible value. The next step is one of comparison. Obviously some of the books already quoted contain comparative material in their illustrations and are also general historical books. This applies particularly to *The Swiss Watch*. Most of the books used for comparison are catalogues either of museum collections or sales. Some of these also contain general information but there are some which are general books on their particular subject. The English long-case and bracket clocks are covered by Cescinsky and Webster in *English Domestic Clocks*. The work of particular makers has been dealt with by R. W. Symons in *Thomas Tompion* (1951) and R. A. Lee, *The Knibb Family, Clockmakers* (1964). For a general coverage of clocks dealing with French clocks in particular, there is nothing to beat *La Pendule Française* produced by Editions Tardy of Paris. This is primarily a picture book with illustrations gathered from a wide variety of sources. It contains quite a lot of technology and some text. Starting with five small volumes which were almost pamphlets it has progressed to three volumes. The first two are on the mainstream French clocks and the third on French provincial clockmaking and the rest of the world. All three volumes are rarely out of print at the same time. New editions are continually in preparation and presumably this will continue as long as the compiler lives. It is virtually indispensable, particularly for the French clocks of the nineteenth century, although the cheaper models have so far been neglected, as have carriage clocks. There are rumours that a specialist book on carriage clocks is in preparation.

As the Scandinavian pieces are sometimes mistakenly attributed to France or even Austria, *Sekler och Sekunder*, published in 1952 by the Nordiska Musee and the catalogue of the Danish Urmuseum at Århus by C. Waagepetersent (1959) can be useful in settling arguments. Unfortunately the catalogue of the Mody Collection of Japanese clocks is virtually unattainable. E. Drummon-Robertson covered Japanese clockmaking in *The Evolution of Clockwork* but as this is sought after for its general historical content, it too is difficult to come by. However, there is *Clocks of Japan* by Professor Ruji Yamaguchi. Although the main text is in Japanese, there is an English introduction. As it was published in 1950, it must be getting scarce enough to be considered an investment.

There are three books on Dutch clockmaking. Two are by W. F. J. Hana, *Klokken* (1961) and *Friesa Klokken* (1964). The third is Spierdijk's *Klokken en Klokkenmakers*.

As far as Italian horology is concerned, there is only one book—*Orologi dal '500 al' '800* by Antonio Simoni. There are plenty of illustrations.

German and Austrian watches and clocks are dealt with by H. Alan Lloyd's *The Book of Old Clocks and Watches*. This is a translation of H. von Bertele's *Uhren*, which aimed at being a new edition of Ernst von Basserman-Jordan's classsic work that failed to hit the target. *Die Uhr* by Anton Lubke also contains a good selection of illustrations.

But before leaving clocks, there are a few other books which deserve mention. *Horlogerie*, the catalogue of the clock and watch section of the Conservatoire des Arts et Métiers in Paris, and *The Long Case Clock* by Eric Bruton. *Horlogerie* is slightly more technical than most catalogues and naturally concentrates on French clocks. It includes a good bibliography of the more advanced French technical books. Eric Bruton's book serves as a good introduction to the less exotic English clock. It has been followed by a second book with a somewhat larger scope, *Clocks and Watches 1400–1900*. The skeleton clock has been rather looked down on by serious collectors except in some particular instances. For this reason the interior decorators have had a field day, largely because they have been dealing almost in bulk with little

A mid-17th Century case more in the tradition of Limoges than Toutin. The design is technically simple but visually effective. The surface is not smooth, but the raised portions seem to be part of the ground rather than the actual colour as in the next watch. The enamel seems to be applied to a copper base.

(£30–300, $85–850)

This case is what is considered to be typical of Blois. There is no really good ground for this belief as there is no evidence that Blois had the monopoly of enamelling during the first half of the 17th Century. The inside of the lid and the centre of the dial are good examples of what can be achieved by laying a single colour in varying thickness to produce the different tones. The outside of the case is basically blue on which the foliage is indicated in black. The actual flowers are added in white blobs with a very slight touch of colour.

(£500–2,000, $1,250–5,600)

An unusual champlevé enamelled case made in the second half of the 17th Century. The surface of the gold case is cut away leaving the design proud, the ground is then filled with white enamel.

(£60–300, $170–850)

Almost certainly French and more likely to be northern than southern. There should be some indication of the maker or place of origin on the base. It is less likely that the movement will be signed. The dating is difficult, 1550–90 is a fairly safe estimate. A later date is possible but it is unlikely that anything survives from an earlier period. The typical two-stage movement can be seen through the glazed sides of the case. The prices of these clocks tends to depend to some extent on the maker and the district, those coming from Blois seem to fetch the higher prices. Ten years ago such a clock would not be likely to pass the £200, $560 mark but today that figure can almost be multiplied by ten.

Not all two-stage movements are French, they were also made in Flanders and England. It would be most exceptional to find a Germanic one and equally exceptional to find one which was hexagonal and not French.

The silver dial decorated with basse-taille enamel should date from the early 17th Century. It is exceptionally difficult, if not impossible, to locate this clock solely on external evidence, it is likely to be Germanic and that includes eastern Switzerland. Because of its size and decoration some serious horologists would regard it as a toy.

(£40–150, $110–450)

Another problem of provenance. This silver cased clock is more likely to be Flemish than anything else. The shape of the aperture for the phases of the moon is unconventional.

(£60–200, $165–550)

Yet another variation of the 'portrait' watch. The miniature is contained in a frame incorporated in a freestanding floral spray mounted over the back of the movement and visible through the glazed back of the gold case. These watches were made during the second half of the 18th Century. Most of the movements have verge escapements but other types can be found. There are signs that the price of these is going up.

(£20–60, $50–170)

The colour of the enamel, the diamond and the unusual engine-turning will somewhat compensate for the small size of this watch but much will depend on the quality of the stone. £150–300, $450–900, if the stone is of top quality and well cut.

The fact that the enamel is inside the case would usually detract from the price but here it is an asset. The miniature depicts Louis XVI saying farewell to his family and would have to be concealed by its Royalist owner. A useful price comparison is impossible and an estimate would only be a guess. This is a watch with great possibilities and would hold whatever price it fetched. The appreciation rate is problematical.

Another Chinese market watch. The movement will not necessarily be the usual Fleurier movement invented by Ilbery but may have a more English look although it was still made in Switzerland. Ilbery's name sometimes adds a small premium but the price will largely depend on the decoration. The design of the case and bow indicate the 1700s.

(£120–350, $360–1,000)

The automaton repeater is, frankly, a novelty but is mildly sought after. The figures either side of the dial strike the bells in synchronisation with the repeating. The small button just on the left of the bottom of the case indicates an automaton scene concealed by the plaque below the dial. The plaque is moved out of the way by sliding the button along the band of the case. The presence of such concealed automata will double the price at least.

(£30–120, $85–350)

thought for technical detail. And because of the expanding market and rising prices, many unsuspected, interesting clocks have come to light. These skeleton clocks provide the subject matter for a book by F. B. Royer-Collard to be published later this year.

For watch collectors the classic book is still G. H. Baillie's *Watches* published in 1929. An expensive book, and a doubtful investment but likely to remain indispensable to the serious investor for many years yet. Equally indispensable, and likely to become a classic is another book with the same title written by Cecil Clutton and George Daniels. Although this provides a general introduction, it goes much further than is customary on the technical side, with particulars of the details which separate seemingly identical watches and can make all the difference between a good and a bad investment. *The Story of Watches* by T. P. Cuss is the best introduction to the novice but copies are hard to find as it has been out of print for many years. However, it will soon be replaced by a new book by the same author. The best of all the catalogues was written by E. Jaquet for the Musée d'Horlogerie de Genève. It is more than just a catalogue as it contains many details not to be found elsewhere. Unfortunately, only 1,000 copies were printed in 1952 and it soon went out of print. It is difficult to understand why it was not reissued. The price of available copies is rising steadily. The catalogue of the horological collections at Besançon has been largely overlooked and has not received the attention it deserves. It does not have as many illustrations as the other catalogues but this is more than compensated for by the excellent 13 page introduction followed by a very brief bibliography with short comments by the author. There can be no complaints about the number of illustrations in the catalogue of the Musée d'Horlogerie at La Chaux-de-Fonds. They certainly outweigh the text which is confined to captions. Some of the illustrations are in colour in the latest edition. The Le Locle catalogue is also full of illustrations. In Paris the bookstall of the Louvre can occasionally be persuaded to disgorge a copy of Gaston Migeon's catalogue of the Paul Garnier collection. Although this was printed in 1917, it is still authoritative and the continued availability is a reflection of the organisation of the Louvre bookstall rather than the value of the book. *English Watches* by J. F. Hayward published by the Victoria and Albert Museum, provides a series of illustrations of English watches in the museum and in addition has reproductions of plates taken from the contemporary design books. These do not duplicate those in *L'Horlogerie Ancienne*. The majority of the illustrations contained in the books so far mentioned are of clocks and watches in public collections and are of interest for comparison with purchases. Catalogues of private collections give information of possible acquisitions. Naturally these include the earlier sale catalogues which are of no real use as a source of prices. This idea has been largely overlooked in the field of horology. Given the catalogue of any collection, it is possible to trace many of the clocks to museums, but some remain unaccounted for. These are still at large and may eventually be for sale. It may take time to locate them but it can and does happen. The trail may be a long one and lead through other collections and catalogues, but the possible dividend can be high enough to warrant the effort. Certain catalogues, like that of the Spitzer Collection, are well known but there are many more to be found in the overlooked bibliographies and footnotes of some of the horological books. The provenance of illustrations in the older books should not be overlooked either. The Olaguer collection was almost entirely dispersed quite recently. This had been catalogued by Luis Montreal under the title *Relojes Antiguos*. Most of the clocks and watches passed into private hands. But these cannot be expected to come on to the market in the immediate future, so the book is to be kept. Dubois's book on the Soltykoff collection has the advantage of being well illustrated and containing quite a good historical section. Some of the clocks and watches may still be at large. Enrico Morpurgo's book, *Precious Watches*, published in 1966 by Omega contains many items from private collections, at least one of which is being dispersed. There are two other books which are valuable for general comparative reference. *The Delle Piane Collection* by Bruno Parisi and *Orologi nel Tempo* by Luigi Pippa. An English edition of the latter is due in 1967. Pippa's book is noteworthy as he gives details of the movements of many of the clocks, a thing most authors are reluctant to do. For the more specialised

A late 18th Century French clock:
Cupid's left hand indicates the time.
(Wallace Collection)

collector the following books will be found to be useful. *Le Monde des Automates* by Chapuis and Gélis, a two volume work published in 1928. This is the definitive work on automata of all kinds and sizes and includes almost everything the horological investor is likely to encounter. Naturally, it is not cheap and has been known to fetch over £100, $280 at auctions. But it can still be considered as an investment as there is no likelihood of a comparable work being produced today. The nearest thing to it is *Automata*, also by Chapuis but this time with Droz and with an English edition. It was intended to take the place of the earlier book, a hopeless task for a single volume, but still a worthwhile book. Another Chapuis book, *Le Montre Chinoise*, is a collectors' item as well as a useful reference book for the decoration of the later Swiss export watches. It is the only book which illustrates the Chinese trade-marks used by some of the various firms. For collectors of the work of A-L. Breguet, Sir David Salomons book *Breguet* is a must. This was published in English

A late 18th Century French gilt bronze clock. *(Wallace Collection)*

An 18th Century French mantel clock.
(Wallace Collection)

In general the French are not particularly
interested in horological details and regard
their clocks as furniture. As such they are
part of the general boom. The price will
depend on the wood and the quality of the
ormolu. If you do decide to buy such a
good look at the movement and make sure
that the original brass cased weights and the
pendulum are still with it as they will be
visible through the glazed base. Replacements are expensive.

The invention of this type of mystery clock is attributed to Robert Houdini who was better known as a conjurer than clockmaker. The movement is contained in the base.
(£60–250, $168–700)

Left

This is a true bracket clock. There can be no doubt that the two belong together. The presence of a musical movement, visible below the dial would add to the price. The great advantage of these clocks is that they need nothing to stand on.
(£120–600, $336–1,680 or higher)

Opposite right

It is a wonder that such clocks got safely to China in the 1780's. It is a greater wonder that they survived the journey back. The truth is that many of them never went. There are still mysteries surrounding the where and how of their production but little doubt about their price: £1,500, $4,200 upwards. There are waterfalls or progressions 'on all floors' to the accompaniment of bells.

in 1921 and was followed by a French edition in 1923 which some people consider to be better. Part of the Salomons collection has been dispersed in three sales held in London (Christies) in 1964/5. Some readers may think it strange that a book on investing should contain so much about books, but there are signs that collectors are becoming both more discriminating and more specialised. In this, they are only following the lead of collectors in other fields where a small difference in colour or design can make a very big difference in price. It cannot be over-emphasised that the really successful investor is the one who is ahead of the field in purchasing trends. You must be able to identify rarities before they are known to be rare and when their price is still low. This can only be accomplished with a certain amount of study of general books and must be done before the specialised books and oeuvre catalogues are written, as has already happened in the case of Breguet, the Knibbs and Tompion whose clocks and watches are usually only the investments of the very rich. Most, but not all of the books already referred to, deal with more decorative aspects of the clock and watch—the case rather than the movement. This is a reflection of the general trend of horological collecting for many years. But the picture has been gradually changing, particularly since publication of *Watches* by Clutton and Daniels, which underlines the importance of certain technical details, especially in the development of the escapement. The specialist in the lever escapement will need *It's about Time* by Paul Chamberlain. Although R. T. Gould's *The Marine Chronometer* deals specifically with the larger machine, it should be consulted for details of escapements and compensation. For the more general introduction to escapements, there is W. J. Gasley's *Clock and Watch Escapements*. But for those going further there is *Echappements* by Charles Gros. This was published in 1913 and is definitely an investor's book. But much of its content is contained in *Les Echappements* by Editions Tardy. Naturally the every-day dictionary rarely covers technical language and horology is not normally included in standard technical dictionaries. There is however, G. A. Berner's *Dictionnaire Professionel Illustré de l'Horlogerie* which is useful for both technical and artistic details providing they are not too antique. Britten's *Watch and Clockmakers' Handbook* (15th edition 1955) can be helpful for the older terms and also contains much other useful technical information. There is one field of horology which has not so far been exploited. It should at least amuse and could be a source of possible profit. This is a search for clocks and watches comparable with those occurring in pictures. A small initial collection of such pictures was assembled by Alfred Chapuis and published in 1954 under the title *De Horologis in Arte*. There is no publication showing prices and market trends in the horological world. Several magazines do quote the current option prices for selected items, but the wise investor will obtain and keep as many priced sales catalogues as he can. Obviously there is a limit to the number of catalogues which can usefully be kept. There is the limitation imposed by space and the problem of indexing. There is no real sense in having more catalogues than can conveniently be referred to. Ten years is about the limit. After that the general catalogues should be weeded out leaving those dealing with complete collections and perhaps the better, illustrated catalogues. These form an investment in themselves but should not be used as guides to price. Under this heading there are the Sarasin collection (Fischer Galleries, Lucerne 1948), the Webster collection (two sales at Sotheby's 1954) and the Antoine-Fiel collection sold by Franz A. Menna in Cologne in 1955. Perhaps the Farouk catalogue (1954) could be added to these as it contains a good selection of decorative and automaton watches. For prices there are in date order, the Bloch-Pementel collection (Hotel Drouot, Paris 1961), the Wheeler collection (Sotheby's 1961), the Dennison collection (Christie's 1961), the Chester Beatty collection (Sotheby's 1962/3) which also included gold boxes, and the Prestige collection of watches (Sotheby's April 1963)—the clocks were sold later the same year in October together with some watches from the Illbert collection, part of the Kalish collection was also sold by Sotheby's in 1964.

It is not claimed that this is a fully comprehensive bibliography. The books have been selected as being of general use for the investor and providing a ready source of comparative material rather than a comprehensive history of the decorative and technical aspects of clock and watch making.

The dial of an early 18th Century French pedestal clock. *(Wallace Collection)*

INDEX